# Anxious Attachment

# Recovery

Restore Confidence, Let Go Of Abandonment
Fears And Build A Path Towards Healthy
Relationships And A Secure Attachment Style

By

**Elara Hayes**

Elara Hayes

# Content

# Your Free Gift

As a way of saying thanks for your purchase, I'm offering the book 'The Five Step Process To Mindful Peace' for FREE to my readers.

**To get instant access just go to:**

https://broadhorizonpublishing.com/elara-free-gift

**Inside the book, you will discover:**

- How to harness the power of mindfulness to achieve inner tranquillity.

- Strategies for overcoming stress and anxiety through simple, daily practices.

- Techniques to cultivate a deeper sense of self-awareness and compassion.

If you want to achieve a more peaceful and centred state of mind, make sure to grab this free book.

# Introduction

# Understanding Anxious Attachment

---

## 1.1 Wolves behind the bush

Have you ever been afraid? No, I am not talking about the rational fear of losing someone. But of a much deeper fear that affects all your relationships and prevents you from fully experiencing them. Perhaps this feeling is a recurring theme in your love stories. Stories that follow the same dull and unchanging script for years.

Your relationship starts on a high note, bringing you joy and happiness, to the point where you say, "Yes, he must be the one!" And yet, after only a few months, uncertainty sets in and fear takes over. What was once pure joy turns into fear—fear of losing the one you love.

Little by little, those affirmations transform into doubts like "Does he really love me?" or "Could he leave me at any moment?"

Perhaps this feeling haunts you in your relationships with friends, family, or in your professional life. It's the same feeling Hamlet described when he said, "I could be bounded in a nutshell and count myself a king of infinite space, were it not that I have bad dreams."

If it is any consolation, you should know that Hamlet struggled with this fear as well. Only he hid it behind grand speeches, which we refer to as *avoidance* in today's clinical jargon. These dysfunctional solutions may appear to address the problem, but they only make it worse.

For example, when faced with the fear of losing someone, you might pretend that nothing has happened. Or you might try to control that fear through jealousy, possessiveness, and constant emotional demands. Sounds familiar?

Instead of solving the problem, these behaviors make it worse over time because they are designed to hide the one question you can't face. It may be a simple question, but it is the key to all psychology:

"Why are you afraid?"

Over the years, you may have given yourself many different answers. You may have told yourself that the fear you feel is justified because human relationships are fragile, and you must do everything you can to keep them alive.

Or perhaps you've tried to hide your feelings because they've always made you feel abnormal and different from others. That's why you've always carried that burden of insecurity to yourself in your relationships (friendships or professional life), which has robbed you of your sleep and given you bad dreams.

I would like to distinguish between what psychologists call *motivated* and *unmotivated* emotions. Imagine walking alone, high up in the mountains, in a forest where you know wolves live.

Suddenly, you hear rustling behind the bushes.

What do you feel? Fear, of course.

In this case, fear is a motivated emotion that has a specific goal in the mechanics of the human organism. Its purpose is to alert you of a dangerous situation and put you in a position to fight or flee.

After a few seconds, you realize there are no ravenous wolves behind the bush, only a small squirrel. The fear naturally disappears. The body gradually regains its balance; your pulse slows down and your muscles become less tense.

There is a structure in our brain called the "amygdala," which has many functions, such as recognizing potential dangers and warning us. In neurological terms, the amygdala has realized that the danger is not real, but imaginary, and has *withdrawn* the emotion of fear.

Let's imagine a second scenario where your partner is out on a business trip. For a day or two, everything seems to go well. But then a certain feeling arises: the fear that the distance between you and your partner means danger, and you worry this distance might mean the end of your love story.

In this case, the fear is irrational since your partner has just called you and everything is going well between you both. Yet, you feel anxious. No matter how hard you try to banish your fear, it is always there, even preventing you from sleeping.

We are dealing with a mechanism that is quite complex and strangely similar to that of panic attacks.

When it comes to the wolves, feeling frightened was justified because of a (dangerous) stimulus. In response to this stimulus, the amygdala produced the emotion of fear. Once the harmlessness of the stimulus was understood, the emotion disappeared.

Now, however, the emotion is associated with a perceived danger that isn't actually there, but it's perceived so strongly that it triggers the emotion.

To return to our metaphor, when you feel this unfounded worry, you continue to fear that there are wolves behind the bushes, even though you just confirmed it was only a small squirrel.

## 1.2 Attachment Theory

Let's go back to our question: "Why are you afraid?"

The answer was provided by a psychologist named John Bowlby in the middle of the last century through his theory of attachment. Bowlby argued that the way we relate to others is influenced by the relationship patterns we experienced in childhood.

Seemingly, there's nothing new about this theory. Wasn't it the ancient Greeks who argued that the faults of fathers were passed on to their children?

Around 1950, Bowlby began to study child psychology. What interested him most was one question: "How can the relationship with parents influence the minds of infants?"

The answer came after years of study and experimentation. Bowlby realized that children tended to develop patterns of internal functioning, starting with their relationships with caregivers, who would follow them into adulthood. This may seem like a complex concept, so I will try to explain it in simple terms.

Let's imagine a child named Mike who grows up with two loving and present parents.

In the first few years of his life, his parents consistently responded to little Mike's needs with consistency and balance. When Mike cries, his parents are there to comfort him. When he needs support, his parents try to make sure that he does not miss out on anything.

Little Mike's desire to explore the world around him is slowly maturing.

Mike is only one and a half years old, and for him, exploring means venturing into the bedroom by standing and crawling. When he encounters "danger" (or what he perceives to be danger), he immediately returns to his mother. She is his *secure base*, where he knows he will find warmth and comfort.

Bowlby noted that this behavior was not only typical of humans but also of macaques, who surprisingly behaved in a similar way.

As the years pass, Mike grows up and becomes an adolescent. This adolescent becomes a man who is self-confident, trusts others, and is capable of having functional relationships based on joy and contentment. Mike is confident that he will always find a safe place with his partner and is not afraid of loss or rejection.

But what if, as a child, Mike had returned to his secure base and found it empty or, worse still, unavailable?

Would Mike still have developed a secure attachment style? Not at all. Our attachment style depends precisely on the relationship we had with our reference figures in childhood.

If, as a child, we saw wolves hiding behind the bushes, we would continue to be suspicious of their presence as adults. Similarly, if our parents did not provide us with a secure base, how can we expect our partner to do so?

In Bowlby's view, certain attachment styles can be distinguished on the basis of the relationship with parental figures and the presence/absence of a **secure base:**

- **Secure attachment style:** trust in the attachment figure and subsequent ability to form healthy relationships

- **Insecure-avoidant attachment style:** having suffered repeated rejection by the attachment figure, the adult avoids forming intimate relationships

- **Insecure-anxious attachment style:** given the instability of the attachment figure, the adult develops anxiety and fear of loss and rejection

It turns out that we have answered the first basic question: "Why are you afraid?" You are afraid because your greatest fear has already come true in a time so distant that it does not even seem real to you.

## 1.3 About this book

Since I began researching this topic after moving back to Seattle, I have devoted my time to looking at the causes and possible treatments for the insecure-anxious attachment style.

This is because it is a problem that is as common as it is painful. It can affect various areas of life, such as family, work, romantic relationships, and social interaction, which often accompanies patients as a life theme from early childhood.

If you are reading this book, you probably already know what I am talking about: the feeling of inferiority, the fear of loss or rejection that drives all your relationships and prevents you from living the life you really want.

What you may not know is that there are solutions to this problem. Cutting-edge treatments such as Cognitive Behavioral Therapy allow for real cognitive *restructuring* of the patient to change his or her attachment style to a more functional one.

I will discuss this throughout this book, exploring what an insecure-anxious attachment style is, how it is maintained, and its implications. You will also find some practical exercises that will help you not only understand the theory but also take a concrete step toward a life of joy and contentment.

After all, change is always possible when you have a strong will.

# Chapter One

# Anxious Attachment in Psychology

## 1.1 A multi-faceted approach

Psychology is a diverse science, and it doesn't limit itself to providing definitions but seeks to study disorders in the concreteness of everyday life. In fact, psychologists draw their treatment hypotheses and research topics from everyday life. I became interested in the insecure-anxious attachment style when I was a young woman intrigued by the world of interpersonal relationships.

At the time, I was in Maine at my family's home. Visiting Maine meant being on vacation and having a lot of free time to pursue my interests and passions. During my stay, I was reading a short story by Edgar Allan Poe called *Berenice*. Like all of Poe's works, this story was characterized by a dark and disturbing atmosphere.

The story tells of the relationship between Egaeus and Berenice.

The two, who are cousins, decide to marry after being in love since childhood. But Egaeus' love for Berenice is not untroubled. He has a real obsession with her, which often leads him to have painful, compulsive thoughts.

When I read this story, I immediately knew where I wanted to focus my professional research. What interested me most was the pain, disguised as compulsion and the need for certainty, that lay behind Egaeus' behavior, as well as that of many people I knew.

This interest has been my profession for many years. I research the mechanisms that cause and nurture the insecure-anxious attachment style, and I also focus on the possible solutions for learning to live a happy and fulfilling life. Mind you, this is not just an issue that affects the romantic sphere, but, as we shall see, a condition that can take different forms and affect different areas of everyday life.

The question that plagued me at the time was: "Why do some people have functional relationships made of joy while others are forced into a relational life of pain and inner suffering?"

It was 1990. A little over twelve years earlier, John Bowlby, the psychologist mentioned earlier, had given an answer that interested me and the many young psychologists entering the world of relationship dysfunction for the first time.

In a nutshell, Bowlby's theory states that the way we relate to others as adults depends on the transactions we had with caregivers, such as our parents, in childhood.

Let me ask you a question: what do you know about parents who read fairy tales to their children in the womb? Some research has shown that a fetus recognizes their parents' voice from the first trimester of pregnancy (Lee & Kisilevsky, 2014) and that this voice can have a significant impact on the healthy growth of the child. This may come as a surprise to you, but it reveals the intimate bond that has existed between parents and children since time immemorial.

Parental love affects us not only on an organic level but in ways that science has yet to fully understand and explain. Perhaps the poet Robert Browning was right when he wrote: "Motherhood: all love begins and ends there."

We could say that the love between parents and children comes even before we are born, and it is then natural that it accompanies us throughout our lives.

While studying Bowlby's theory, I came across the concept of the "secure base." This concept was actually developed by a colleague of Bowlby's, a developmental psychologist called Mary Ainsworth. According to Ainsworth, when we are very young (from birth and throughout the first year of life), we are naturally inclined to identify a reference figure. This figure tends to make us feel safe and protected from external dangers and potential obstacles that may come our way.

The presence of a secure psychological and geographical base helps us explore the world around us with serenity. In other words, if the child is secure in the parental figure, they can venture out to discover the world around them with joy and, above all, without fear of abandonment.

But do all children have a secure base? Far from it. When young children grow up with absent or ambivalent parents, they develop a fear of abandonment from a very early age. Here, they can only leave their geographical reference point (the parent) with great anxiety because they are not sure they will find it again when they return from exploring (insecure base).

Mary Ainsworth sought to understand the workings of this mechanism. She devised an experimental paradigm (an experiment) to investigate the quality and pattern of this parent-child interaction.

Her question was: "How does the relationship with the parent during the first years of life influence the child's attachment style?"

**Her conclusions were:**

- A child (Joe) who develops a **secure attachment** has parents who inspire trust. Joe will, therefore, involve his mother in exploring his environment (showing her his toys and interacting with her). When the mother is absent, Joe cries. However, when she returns, he greets her calmly and continues to play.

- A child (Emily) who develops an **insecure-avoidant attachment** has parents who are absent and do not provide a secure base (e.g., they complain when the baby cries). For this reason, Emily tends to show no interest in the mother and explores the environment without involving her. Emily will remain indifferent even when the mother leaves and returns.

- A child (Ann) who develops an **insecure-anxious attachment** has parents whose behavior is ambivalent, sometimes giving and sometimes withholding attention. In this way, Ann doesn't pay attention to her environment because she is too busy looking for her mother's gaze. When the mother leaves, Ann begins to cry uncontrollably and continues to cry even when she returns.

Going back to the basic concept, we can say that Joe has a secure base; Emily has an insecure base and reacts by avoiding it; Ann has an insecure base and reacts by developing deep anxiety and fear of abandonment.

We will discuss the prototype of this third child (Ann) later in this book.

## 1.2 From childhood to adulthood

Memory is an ambiguous thing. We probably remember little or nothing of our childhood. What we do remember is often altered by long processes of re-evaluation, symbolization, and falsification of memories.

For example, if I were to ask you what your first memory was, you might dig into the depths of your memory. You would probably try to go back to your earliest childhood years and either find nothing or rely on hazy, evocative images.

According to various scientific studies, conscious memories do not begin to form until the age of two (Peterson, 2021). And this is where the ambiguity of memory lies: the things we do not remember, or rather cannot remember, are precisely those that have left an indelible mark on us. A trace that we are still struggling to get rid of.

Let us return to Mary Ainsworth and her theory of attachment.

What does this theory say? Not only do children develop attachment styles depending on their relationship with their parents (and thus with their secure base), but these attachment styles also become internal models that continue to function as children grow into adulthood.

An internal model is a mental schema that each individual constructs, a kind of map that represents him or herself in relation to others.

To use a metaphor, we could say that attachment styles are like internal stamps: no matter how hard we try to use a stamp differently, it will always leave the same mark on the paper.

The same thing happens with attachment styles: no matter how many relationships you have, if you have developed an insecure-anxious attachment style, you will have different relationships, but they will always *feel* the same. Because in all of them, you will leave the indelible mark of your pain and the wounds that go back to early childhood.

But how exactly does the insecure-anxious attachment style work?

As I said, I have dealt with this problem many times in my research, and it is chameleon-like and multi-faceted. The symptoms can indeed appear as those of a generalized anxiety disorder, but they are projected onto interpersonal relationships.

In general, an adult with an insecure-anxious attachment style is afraid of abandonment or of not being enough (of not being loved) because they felt this way as a child when they could not find a secure base.

**Therefore, the most obvious signs may be:**

- Fear of abandonment

- Fear of not measuring up

- Fear of losing loved ones

- Anxiety disorders

- A desire for constant intimacy with the partner

**In the face of these signals, the subject tends to engage in much the same dysfunctional behavior:**

- Reacts to the fear of abandonment with jealousy

- Acts possessive or makes constant emotional demands

- Responds to fear of not measuring up with compensatory tools, such as the need for external validation (especially in professional relationships)

- Establishes friendship, romantic, and family relationships under the banner of need and emotional dependency

All these behaviors are nothing more than *defense mechanisms*. Mechanisms to simulate the truth of things that, over time, make the clinical problem worse and cause personal, relational, and social problems.

In what sense?

In the sense that a person with an insecure-anxious attachment doesn't feel jealousy or a desire to possess their partner. They don't need external validation from their employer or colleagues. In psychology, these feelings are called *parasitic emotions,* meaning they mask the natural emotion because it's too painful to accept and process.

Here's an example to explain this concept: I have a fight with a friend, and I feel sad. To express my sadness, I use anger (because that is what I am used to, or I am simply led by my inability to get in touch with my emotions). In this case, sadness is the natural emotion, while anger is the parasitic emotion.

Similarly, in a romantic relationship, an adult with insecure-anxious attachment feels sadness rather than jealousy. This sadness is a radical and atavistic pain that arises from not feeling loved by their parental figures. A pain that is expressed through parasitic emotions, which functions to hide the natural emotion that would be too intense and painful for them.

Through a strange dysfunctional mechanism, the brain, instead of letting the pain out, covers it up with jealousy, possessiveness, and the need for external validation. This defense mechanism is a natural reaction of the brain trying to protect itself, but it ends up causing even more damage than good.

Confronting and acknowledging the pain is the first step in freeing ourselves from the ghosts we too often carry around with us. As long as we keep hiding the truth, we can only go around in circles, like tops gone mad. Don't worry, we'll discuss this topic in greater detail later.

## 1.3 General Anxiety or Anxious Attachment?

Back to us.

Some time ago, a friend of mine told me a strange story. She had experienced it firsthand in the 1990s in downtown New York.

To make a long story short, my friend (let's call her L.) was standing on the street outside a café she frequented on the Upper East Side. Suddenly, she heard screams coming from a car parked a short distance away. Terrified, L. approached the car and saw a young girl (whom we will call G.) in her early twenties emerge from it.

The girl looked very upset, as if she had just fought with her boyfriend or something. Since the young woman would not stop crying, L. asked her if she wanted to have coffee. After some hesitation, the girl agreed. So, they went to a French café on the Upper East Side and had a conversation that went like this:

*L.: What happened?*

*G.: I had a fight with my boyfriend.*

*L.: And why did you fight with him?*

*G.: He doesn't understand. He doesn't understand anything!*

*L.: What does he not understand?*

*G.: My fear! I feel anxious when he goes out with his friends, but not because I'm jealous. I swear I'm not jealous! But I get overwhelmed with fear. The same anxiety I get when I know I have an exam at university. He keeps saying that he does not understand me, that jealousy is unbearable for him...*

A long time later, my friend told me the same story (in other words, of course). She suffered from insecure-anxious attachment, and after her therapist's initial diagnosis, she thought of this encounter because it reminded her of the feelings she had experienced in romantic relationships.

Of course, it is impossible to make a diagnosis from a distance, but from the girl's words, I can deduce that her problem was generalized anxiety rather than an insecure-anxious attachment style. As I said, the two disorders are often confused, making distinguishing between them difficult. But what is the real difference between anxiety spectrum disorder and insecure-anxious attachment?

An experiment conducted in 2023 analyzed the case of Fred, a twenty-eight-year-old man, who consulted a psychologist to address issues that prevented him from dealing with interpersonal relationships with composure (Garnier and Stuart (2023). Specifically, Fred suffered from anxiety disorders that forced him to end his relationship to escape the oppressive feelings he was experiencing.

Fred constantly worried about his partner's physical safety. This anxiety was not only psychological but also somatic, causing him sleep disturbances, muscular tension, general malaise, and depressive episodes. It was not uncommon for Fred to go to his partner's house during the night to make sure she was okay (e.g., that she did not suddenly become ill, etc.). However, his anxiety was not only about his partner but more generally about all occasions of daily life.

When Fred met his partner, he felt the need to organize appointments in detail in order to avoid unplanned and potentially dangerous situations. In the long run, Fred had come to a conclusion: he had to end his relationship with his partner, or his clinical condition would worsen.

But how does Fred's case differ from a patient with insecure-anxious attachment?

On closer inspection, his distress is not caused by fear of

abandonment but by fear without an objective referent, typical of generalized anxiety disorder. On the other hand, the cause of Fred's behavior is not a dysfunctional relationship with the parental figure (with the absence of a secure base) but a traumatic experience he had as a child.

As a child, Fred was forced to spend a large part of his time providing physical care and psychological support to his mother, who was weak in both respects. In his case, the trauma thus caused a deep irrational fear that eventually permeated all his intimate relationships and expressed itself in the enactment of compulsions aimed at alleviating the anxious stimulus.

**This is how generalized anxiety works:**

- A past experience (often a trauma) leaves a deep wound in the individual

- This wound, unhealed, causes generalized anxiety and distress

- The anxiety is then discharged through compulsive attitudes (in Fred's clinical case, excessive worrying and caring behavior toward his partner), which are tasked to soothe the anxious stimulus

There are, therefore, differences between generalized anxiety and the anxious-insecure attachment styles in terms of the content of the irrational fear and the aetiology. Whereas the insecure attachment style is caused by a dysfunctional relationship with attachment figures, generalized anxiety may be caused by environmental (e.g., past trauma), genetic, and personality factors that do not necessarily involve parental figures.

For example, a particularly violent trauma, such as abuse or bereavement occurring late in life, may be the cause of generalized anxiety, but cannot, according to Bowlby's theory, be the cause of an anxious-insecure attachment style.

Furthermore, generalized anxiety has a general content and serves as a psychosomatic explanation for a traumatic experience or a deep-seated malaise. On the other hand, the anxious-insecure attachment style serves as an expression of the emotional wound experienced when one has not felt love and security from parental figures.

**The DSM-5 (APA, 2022) defines the diagnostic criteria for generalized anxiety as follows:**

- Anxiety must be chronic, lasting more than six months

- Physical symptoms (insomnia, restlessness, muscle

tension) are present

- The most common dysfunctional strategy is avoidance (avoiding situations that might cause anxiety)

Now that we know how to distinguish between the two disorders, we can delve deeper into the anxious-insecure attachment style by talking about internal patterns and how they are conceptualized in behavioral psychology.

# 1.4 Internal working models and their meaning

At this point you might say: "Put simply, attachment theory says that our relationships are influenced by the relationship we had with our parents." Of course, this is true, but it is an oversimplification from a theoretical point of view. In order to really understand attachment theory, we need to clarify the workings of the inner models that Mary Ainsworth talks about.

What exactly is an internal model?

Let us begin by saying that the theories from Bowlby and Ainsworth owe much to behaviorist psychology.

This school of thought grew out of the research of Ivan Pavlov, a Russian physician and physiologist, who was interested in how living beings learn and develop from their interaction with the environment.

To explore this idea, Pavlov studied the behavior of dogs (subjects) when confronted with food (unconditioned stimulus). At the mere sight of food, the dog would begin to salivate, which is known as mouthwatering. Now, when Pavlov presented the dogs with food, he simultaneously administered the sound of a small bell (conditioned stimulus). Over time, the dogs learned to associate the sound of the bell with the imminent arrival of food, so they began to salivate in the absence of food and in the presence of the unconditioned stimulus.

Pavlov's theory soon spread around the world, eventually influencing the work of the American psychologist F. B. Skinner, considered the father of behaviorism.

**Skinner's idea was something like this:**

- By using stimuli, it's possible to condition the behavior of living beings (classical Pavlovian conditioning).

- Additionally, it is also possible to strengthen or weaken a particular behavior through the stimuli themselves.

This is the *theory of reinforcement*. It works like this: if I want to encourage a child to behave in a certain way, such as studying, I will reward them every time they meet my expectations. The reward will ensure that the child learns the behavior in the long term.

As a result, the child will think: "When I study (behavior), I get a reward (reinforcement); I will then continue to study (reinforced behavior) to get the reward again."

The same goes for the opposite. If I want to inhibit a certain behavior, I will give a punishment instead of a reward. Is this not what we all do with our children and in every area of our lives?

In the office, if we work consistently and efficiently, we get promoted (rewarded). So, we tend to work in the same way to get the same kind of reward in the future. Conversely, if we are always absent, do not complete our tasks, and are easily distracted, we may be fired (punishment) or suffer other sanctions.

Reinforcement theory is thus based on classical conditioning but goes further to modify the individual's decision-making style.

One interesting example is gambling, which uses intermittent reinforcement. If I play a slot machine, I may lose several rounds in a row. Eventually, the structure of the machine will lead me to at least one win (prize). I will then be inclined to play again in the hope of getting that prize again.

The argument could also be extended to social networks (this is the purpose of "likes" on Facebook and Instagram) and certain manipulation techniques such as love bombing. The narcissist using this technique initially gives a lot of attention (reward) and then takes it away (punishment). The victim of the manipulator will, therefore, be inclined to do whatever it takes to get the reward instead of the punishment.

What does this have to do with our discussion?

Skinner's theory was fundamental to Bowlby's research. However, unlike Skinner, Bowlby did not believe that the dynamics of reinforcement could only enhance or inhibit behavior but that it had effects on the mental structure of the individual.

Let us return to the parent-child relationship.

According to reinforcement theory, if I grow up with a parent who is not a secure base for me, I should be strongly inclined to emulate the behavior of the secure base. Put **simply:**

- I know that my behavior will not affect the amount of love I receive (from the parent);

- therefore (as an adult), I avoid loving relationships that I tend to regard as useless in the dynamics of affection.

However, psychological research over the last half-century has changed the game. We now know that if I have an avoidant parent, not only can I develop the same form of behavior, but I can also grow up with an anxious-insecure attachment style as a response to the deep emotional pain of rejection I experienced as a child.

Similarly, it has long been known that those who grow up with parents with sadistic personality disorder do not necessarily become sadistic (as is the case with most serial killers). They may also develop problems of emotional dependency on sadistic figures (masochism) or, alternatively, avoid any interpersonal relationship so as not to risk encountering the same figure.

In other words, the conditioning we undergo in childhood is not limited to imprinting a certain type of behavior in us, but it also influences the way we see the world around us.

So, if I grow up with a parent who is not a secure base, I will introject the belief that no individual can truly be a secure base. We are faced with the definition of an internal model or mental schema: a functional or dysfunctional lens through which I view the world.

According to behaviorist theory, and specifically cognitive

behavioral therapy, the cognitive schema is believed to have the power to influence my behavior. These behaviors then affect my daily life and lead me to develop dysfunctional relationships based on, for example, need and dependency.

This is because, influenced by a traumatic stimulus (the behavior of my parents during childhood), I will tend to act out the same response when confronted with all those stimuli that have similarities to the traumatic stimulus (e.g., relationship with a partner, etc.). This explains why, in Bowlby's theory, growing up with an ambivalent parent can lead to the development of an insecure-anxious attachment style in adulthood.

The attachment style is nothing more than my standardized response to an anxiety that is not really about the present relationship but about past pain.

## 1.5 Treatment options and genetic hypotheses

Now we know exactly what the aetiology of the disorder is. It is true that the attachment style we adopt in adulthood depends on the quality of our relationship with our parents (especially, in Bowlby's theory, with our mother).

But if we know the cause of the problem, we can also formulate therapeutic hypotheses. We will discuss these hypotheses in more detail in the final chapter devoted to functional solutions. For now, we'll go over a few details.

Modern psychology has made great progress in recent years. Once we understand the dysfunctional mechanism underlying anxious-insecure attachment, we can act on it using a variety of approaches and theoretical models.

Skinner's theories, for example, have led us to realize that if we expose an individual to an "unwelcome" (anxiogenic) stimulus and get them to associate it with something positive, we can gradually reduce their fear of the stimulus itself.

This assumption is the basis of the practice known as systematic desensitization. This is a method specific to cognitive behavioral therapy that aims to change a patient's response to a particular stimulus by making them perceive it as less dangerous. We will see how it works in more detail below.

**Other treatment hypotheses may include:**

- Interventions aimed at modifying the patient's cognitive patterns, e.g., through the use of verbal therapy and analysis of the patient's history (cognitive restructuring)

- Behavioral changes that may also have a long-term effect

on cognitive schemas (short-term strategic therapy)

- Work on emotional intelligence

- The use of functional solutions to replace the dysfunctional ones implemented by the patient

In this regard, it is known that patients with insecure-anxious attachment can adopt three basic coping styles. By coping style here, we mean dysfunctional behavior of a compulsive nature aimed at managing anxiety caused by a stimulus.

For example, if I perceive a fear of abandonment (stimulus) in a relationship, I may use possessive behaviors such as jealousy and control (dysfunctional, obsessive behavior = coping style) to ward off the fear of abandonment.

These behaviors may provide relief in the short term, but over time, they only exacerbate the clinical picture. Indeed, as we will see in Chapter Four, the human brain tends to modify itself on the basis of our behavior (neural plasticity); in this case not only standardizing dysfunctional solutions but also making anxiogenic thinking more intrusive.

**In terms of cognitive restructuring, dealing with an insecure-anxious attachment style might involve the following steps:**

- Identifying and analyzing the patient's dysfunctional

thought patterns (my mother was ambivalent, and so will all the people in my life)

- Modifying these thought patterns

- Helping to distinguish motivated emotions from those that are unmotivated or related to past traumas

Having reached this point, we need to make a clarification. According to some genetic theories, attachment style is not exclusively due to the relationship with parental figures but to hereditary factors such as DNA transmission. If this were true, it would contradict Bowlby's theory.

The fundamental question is: are people and their behavior the result of genetic inheritance or the influence of the environment (past traumas, relationships with caregivers, etc.)? In other words, if I develop an insecure-anxious attachment, is it because this attachment style is implicit in my DNA or because I am prone to it due to a lack of a secure base?

The hypothesis of this interaction has been the subject of many studies, mainly focusing on pairs of identical twins raised in different families. By studying these subjects, researchers have been able to get their hands on a perfect combination of factors: the twins' genetic makeup was the same, but the environment in which they were raised was different.

One such experiment was carried out in Madrid on a population of 80 homozygotic twins (physically and genetically identical) aged between 3 and 74 (Qi, 2006).

The results were surprising. The DNA of pairs of twins older than 28 years showed more marked differences than those of younger twins. This meant that the interaction with the environment was able to influence the inherited genes. In fact, the most pronounced differences were observed in twins who grew up in different environments.

This study suggests that our character certainly depends on genetic factors but that these factors can, in turn, be influenced by interaction with the environment.

In terms of attachment style, research suggests that we are partly predisposed to develop a certain pattern of behavior because it is implicit in our DNA, but that our DNA can change based on the stimuli we encounter along the way.

The environment can, therefore, cause a gradual change in my basic character, which can have both negative (development of psychopathology) and positive effects (possibility of redefining dysfunctional behavior for a better quality of life).

Try to think for a moment about how you see yourself now and how you saw yourself a few years ago. Surely, you feel that you have changed. You have a different way of looking at the world, at yourself, at your interpersonal relationships.

This perception seems to be justified by scientific research; through your experiences every day, your way of thinking and behaving gradually changes to cope with the different obstacles you encounter on your path. It is no coincidence that the basic assumption of behaviorist psychology is that change is always possible because modifying one's interaction with the environment can alter one's mental makeup. In other words, by working on the way you think, you can change the way you behave and the way you feel (cognitive behavioral therapy). At the same time, by changing the way you behave, it is possible to work on the way you think and therefore the way you feel (short-term strategic therapy).

Now that you have an overview of the topic, we can go further and look at the insecure-anxious attachment style in more detail. In the next chapter, we will discuss how this attachment style manifests itself in romantic relationships and provide some valuable tips for dealing with and overcoming it.

# Chapter Two

# Anxious Attachment Style and Interpersonal Relationships

## 2.1 The anxious mind

In the previous chapter, we analyzed in detail the causes of insecure-anxious attachment and we recognized that the relationship with our parents plays a fundamental role in shaping our worldview.

For twentieth-century German philosophers, the concept of having a worldview had a precise name: *Weltanschauung*. This term refers to the way individuals perceive reality through their senses. And it is precisely because we are talking about "reality" and "senses" that this perspective cannot be confined to just one sphere of life but must encompass them all.

The nineteenth-century philosopher Immanuel Kant, in his famous book *Critique of Pure Reason*, used the metaphor of blue glasses to explain the nature of what he calls "phenomenon."

This concept refers to the reality we perceive through sight. Kant suggested that if we all wore blue-lensed glasses all the time (without even knowing it), we would think that blue is the only existing color.

Similarly, if we were to look at human relationships through the filter of "fear" or "anxiety," we would end up viewing all interpersonal relationships in this way, whether they are romantic, friendship, or professional.

Carl Jung spoke a great deal about worldview in psychology. He believed that in order to put an end to an individual's psychological suffering, it is necessary to make changes in his or her worldview, rather than just focusing on one area of their life. Only in this way can the conflict, which explicitly concerns a single sphere, be resolved.

However, it is not wrong to say that the anxious-insecure attachment style primarily concerns romantic relationships, because it is in this type of relationship that the dynamic of need and desire is most clearly and strongly expressed. If we feel nostalgia or sadness for a friend whom we have not seen for a day or two, this "nostalgia" takes on a more definite and dramatic character in relation to a partner: it becomes pain, like that caused by a wound.

Moreover, in romantic relationships, the element of love is

central and is defined precisely by the relationship with the secure base. In childhood, we sought the support of our mother or father to explore the world. Similarly, as adults, we seek the same kind of support from our partners.

Some time ago, as I listened to my friend Ann (we will call her that to protect her personal identity) talk about her relationship, I noticed similarities with the subject I was studying. At the time, she had been in a relationship with a man for three years. However, she had difficulty in defining the nature of their relationship as he was becoming more distant and cold with each passing day.

Ann had met him three years earlier at a university party organized by a friend. Max (the boyfriend) was the only boy in the group she didn't know. She felt as if she had never seen him before. It was love at first sight between them and they spent most of the evening chatting.

After the first period of dating, Ann seemed to have realized that Max was a rather closed and emotionally reserved guy. She didn't know about his past because he didn't like to talk about it. He had a few girlfriends before her, but he deemed them "unimportant."

Over time, the more Ann tried to break down the wall Max had built between them, the thicker and more impenetrable it became. For example, Max would often cancel a date with her, saying he needed time to study.

Ann, for her part, became more and more anxious, and when Max did not answer her mobile phone, her sense of anxiety grew. She often compulsively checked her phone in the company of her friends, hoping he would call. She was no longer the same: Max's fickleness had brought out an insecurity and jealousy that none of her friends had ever seen in her. What did Max do when he wasn't with her? Did he really spend his afternoons studying, as he told her, or was he hiding something? More importantly, was he planning to leave her at any moment?

This was the situation my friend was in at the time. She told me every detail of it, believing that the problem lay with Max, who was so elusive and apathetic. According to her, he was unaware of the damage he was doing to her.

It is important to note that sometimes the partner triggers these mechanisms. In psychology, there is a category of manipulative behavior aimed at the emotional exploitation of others known as "narcissism." It is not uncommon for pathological narcissists to engage in a kind of *love bombing* with their partners. This involves initially giving them a lot of attention and displays of love, only to withdraw it completely, leaving the partner confused and astonished.

What happens in these cases? Partners who are unaware of this "sadistic" dynamic will try to regain the narcissist's attention and love, further feeding his or her ego and sense of power.

This sets up a pathological mechanism between the dependent and the narcissist. The dependent needs the love of the narcissist and will do anything to get it, and the narcissist needs the love of the dependent to get constant reassurance of his or her "worth."

Talking to Ann, I soon realized that the mechanisms at work between her and her boyfriend were not about narcissism but about insecure-anxious attachment. Ann then shared with me a fragment of the conversation she had with her therapist, whom we will call T.

*T: Tell me about your relationship with your mother. Do you get on well?*

*A: Yes. My mother and I get on well. We talk on the phone once a week.*

*T: And if you had to describe your relationship in one word, what would it be?*

*A: One word… let me think. Maybe it would be "companionship."*

*T: Why did you think of that word?*

*[…]*

Through this conversation, Ann's therapist was trying to make her aware of her clinical picture. At this delicate stage, the therapist must be very careful not to make the patient feel judged; otherwise, they will be discouraged from continuing the process.

Curious as to how the session had gone, I asked Ann to explain the meaning she attached to the word "companionship." Ann explained that when she visited her mother, they sometimes went shopping together, helped her with the housework, or accompanied her to the doctor.

Listening to her, I got the impression that she did not see her mother as a real figure of reference to whom she could turn in times of crisis. It turned out that her mother hardly knew who Max was and that she had never shown too much interest in her daughter's private life, reserving it for more "practical" matters: Ann's studies, her physical health, and her financial situation.

After collecting the material, I returned to my studies and made a list of her dysfunctional behaviors based on what she had told me on various occasions and what I had been able to witness for myself. In psychology, any behavior is often indicative of a "belief" pattern, which is not always rationally recognized by the person performing it. For example, we have discussed how sadness is often disguised as anger and grief as jealousy.

In Ann's case, here is the thought pattern that emerged from my analysis of her case in relation to Max:

| Behavior | Belief |
|---|---|
| I call him several times a day, often asking where he is and who he is with. I pretend to be relaxed and ask him to send me a photo. | I think he is lying to me and avoiding me because he doesn't want to spend time with me. |
| I avoid making plans with my friends if I have any doubts that Max might get out of his "schedule." | If I am always available, he will understand my need to be close to him. |
| I get angry when he cancels on me, and I tell him that he's made me feel bad. | If I make him feel guilty, he will change his mind and spend the day with me. |
| I ask him whether he finds that female friend of his attractive or charming, and what he thinks of her in relation to me. | I don't feel beautiful, intelligent, or desirable, so I seek constant reassurance. |

As Ann's table shows, many of her behaviors were aimed at establishing emotional contact with Max without her being aware of it. Are they not very reminiscent of a child's protest behavior (crying, whining) when they don't get their mother's attention? Many adults who have developed an insecure-anxious attachment will similarly try to get closer to the shrewish partner, often causing them to move further away.

And these are just some of the thoughts that were going through Ann's mind at the time that I was able to identify by talking to her. Who knows how much more pain she was hiding under a false smile!

## 2.2. Anxious-insecure symptomatology and romantic relationships

Ann and I have been friends for a long time, and although you can never say you know people inside out, one thing I know for sure is that I didn't think she was the jealous type. I always thought she was a carefree and confident person. For this reason, I soon became convinced of the existence of one particular factor in her relationship with Max that had brought out this "new" nature in her that was not new at all: insecurity.

Let me explain. Because the person with insecure-anxious attachment constantly lives with the insecurity that the partner does not love them (as Ann did with Max), they will constantly try to implement strategies, called *activating or attachment strategies*, aimed at finding a glimmer of security in the relationship (Shaver

& Mikulincer, 2007).

In short, since the partner does not provide any kind of certainty in the relationship, it is the anxious subject who feeds their own mental structures/schemas through specific thoughts.

Often, these strategies are intrusive thoughts that don't reflect reality and further feed the vicious cycle of anxious attachment. In a sense, they are the foundation, the matrix of the mental belief-behavior pattern that initiates the attachment system.

**Some of the most common activating strategies in romantic relationships with insecure-anxious attachment are:**

- Thinking about the partner all the time

- Believing that being with the partner in question is the only way to love and be loved

- Thinking that the partner's and other people's qualities outweigh one's own (sense of inferiority)

- Underestimating the nature of one's attachment and attributing it to a natural phase of love

- Justifying the partner's negative actions (such as cheating, lying, etc.)

- Always putting the partner in a good light

- Convincing oneself that the partner will change

Since these thoughts have no counterpart in reality, the anxious subject still asserts them through the protest behaviors mentioned earlier.

**To put the pieces of this mental puzzle together, this is what happens:**

*I believe that my partner is my only chance to love and be loved (activating strategy). Therefore, if I always make myself available, he will understand my need to be close to him (belief). Consequently, I avoid making plans with my friends in case my partner is available (behavior).*

Or *I think my partner is smarter than me and his qualities are far superior to mine (activating strategy). As a result, he will have high standards of beauty and intelligence that I will certainly not reach (belief). For this reason, I constantly need reassurance by asking him if he finds a friend he often meets attractive or charming (behavior or protest behavior).*

But what is the unconscious aim of this mental construction? In the eyes of the insecure-anxious subject, it is certainly to seek and simulate closeness with their partner. The act of reassurance by the partner has the effect of calming the attachment system. The biggest problem is when this reassurance does not come.

In the case of insecure-avoidant partners (as in Max's case) who tend to respond to these manifestations of need with indifference, the insecure-anxious person's anxiety does not diminish. On the contrary, it increases disproportionately.

What is at the root of this anxiety that endlessly feeds the attachment mechanism? As we have said, it all starts with the need for certainty intrinsic to every human being. In fact, it is inherent in the psychology of every living being.

Our ancestors, as well as all other living species, have constantly searched for certainty every second of their existence. Searching for food, finding a mate, seeking shelter from the elements: these are all actions aimed at establishing certainty about the continuation of one's species. This is a primary biological need that is a real driving force in the lives of humans and animals.

Not even the advent of culture has been able to alleviate this need. Throughout our lives, we continue to seek all kinds of certainty, including economic stability (studying, working), romantic stability (changing several partners until we find "the right one"), and physical health (the certainty of not falling ill and staying healthy). In short, certainty underpins our biology and culture (Kampourakis et al., 2019).

It's only natural to expect a degree of certainty in our relationship with our partner. We want to know that we are loved, that we can count on them in times of need, and that the trust we place in them will not be betrayed. But the main reason why living beings struggle so hard for this certainty is that the world is governed by precisely the opposite force: uncertainty and precariousness.

In short, we can never predict what will happen in life. Even the very act of walking down the street can hide dangers and pitfalls (traffic accidents, thunderstorms that take us by surprise) as well as good things (finding money on the sidewalk).

In this context, the psychiatrist Daniel Siegel coined the term "temporal integration" to describe the capacity that every human being should develop to allow these two extremes to coexist in their thinking: the awareness of the uncertainty of the world and the human tendency to always seek certainty (Siegel, 2018).

The existence of these two opposing and complementary systems should provide a kind of reassurance to the individual, leading them to think: "In a world dominated by unpredictability, I will do my best to conquer my own personal certainty, even though I know that my search will often be hindered by events beyond my control."

Given this mechanism, how do we fit the psychological profile of the insecure-anxious individual?

Let's think of Ann, who seems to have difficulty accepting this dualism. The awareness of this constant uncertainty causes stress and anxiety in the individual, which they will try to overcome by using classic protest behavior.

For this reason, it is necessary for the insecure-anxious subject to understand this mechanism, along with another fundamental truth: the lack of absolute certainty and the simultaneous need for reassurance must not compromise their chances of experiencing happy and satisfying romantic relationships.

On the contrary, sensitive people like them should try to establish a relationship with a person who has developed a secure attachment. Someone who is not afraid to provide reassurance at the beginning of the relationship, to show themselves available, and to be loving. This is one of the only ways to "break" the vicious circle of the insecure-anxious person who, in time, will have acquired a solid enough foundation, reducing their need for constant reassurance from their partner.

In this way, the anxious, insecure person slowly gains a new confidence in themselves and their secure base. They will realize that a momentary estrangement on the part of their partner (an outing with friends or a business trip) does not mean the end of their love affair. As a result, even the insecure and anxious person will feel calm enough to go about their activities (meeting friends or concentrating on work) without spending all their mental energy trying to repair the relationship.

In Chapter Six, we will discuss in more detail how to make one's partner aware of these needs without getting caught up in the vortex of the attachment system. We will do this by introducing some of the basic techniques for cultivating an effective and conscious communication style.

## 2.3. Is it only about love?

"Thinking about your partner all the time and not being able to concentrate on anything else." Does this sound familiar?

It is one of the activating strategies we listed in the previous paragraph, one of those intrusive thoughts that trigger the vicious cycle of the attachment system.

When a thought becomes intrusive, it inevitably tends to occupy our minds constantly, making it difficult for us to devote our energies to other activities. Indeed, it is not uncommon to hear of people at work who always have one eye on their mobile phone screen to see if their partner has contacted them.

But it doesn't stop there. In fact, one of the most common behaviors of these people is to externalize this "obsession" in other ways. This often takes the form of talking to their friends about their partner (as Ann often did with me and constantly asking for advice on how to deal with the situation.

This behavior, together with the constant attempt to seek emotional and physical contact with the partner, only ensures that the partner is always present in the lives and minds of those who evoke them, even in their absence.

Obviously, all this stress plays an extremely negative role in the other areas of the insecure-anxious subject's life. Imagine for a moment that you have to go to work and you spend the whole day, from morning to evening, with one fixed thought in your head: "Did I turn off the burner after making breakfast?" So, you try to calm yourself down, and you tell yourself that this is just your paranoia without any basis: "It's never happened before that I forgot to turn off the gas, so why should it happen today?" But nothing, your sixth sense just won't let you rest, and you can't think of anything else….

The intrusive thinking of an insecure-anxious person works more or less in the same way: Until they get reassurance about their paranoia, they can't find peace and concentrate on anything else.

These feelings that plague the private life of an insecure-anxious person are the same ones that make their working life hostile and unpleasant. Just as they tend to overestimate their partners and underestimate themselves, the same happens at work. The insecure-anxious have a very high opinion of their colleagues but not of themselves, and they do not speak openly about their opinions when they differ from those of the majority. In addition, they are generally more susceptible to stress (Jiang et al., 2019).

Doesn't this read like a fitting example of the blue-glasses metaphor? It seems that a person who has developed feelings of low self-esteem and inferiority in relation to what they think of their partner will harbor the same feelings in the work sphere, preventing them from achieving goals that make them feel satisfied and fulfilled.

There is more. Recently, more and more researchers have been focusing on the phenomenon of *workplace deviance*, which is the tendency of some employees to sabotage their own company by engaging in certain behaviors. **Some of the most common are:**

- Being late for work or lingering during the daily break;

- Arguing frequently with colleagues

- Failing to complete tasks or completing them in a slow and disorganized manner

- Wasting company resources; stealing or sabotaging company property or equipment.

What has all this got to do with our book? Recently, some research has suggested that typical workplace deviant behavior is also observed in employees who have an insecure-anxious attachment.

One such study was conducted by Weijiao Ye and colleagues (2022) and published in the prestigious journal *Frontiers in Psychology*. The researchers administered questionnaires to a total of 442 Chinese office workers, asking them to rate the truthfulness of certain personal statements on a scale of **1 to 7, such as:**

- "I often look to my partner for reassurance without receiving it."

- "My need for affection sometimes frightens people."

- "I often fear that my partner does not care for me as much as I care for him/her."

And other information related to work and the professional sphere, previously used in questionnaires measuring deviant behavior at work, **such as:**

- "I often take long breaks at work without permission."

- "I do not respect my work environment."

- "I spend a lot of time fantasizing about other things during my working hours."

It is important to note that the questionnaires were sent out at different times and in different ways for each participant to prevent them from guessing the purpose of the research. For example, a participant might receive the attachment questionnaire by email and then, some time later, the questionnaire about self-perception at work by text message. The results of their survey showed that those who showed signs of attachment anxiety also showed signs of deviant behavior at work.

In short, it seems that people who lacked a secure foundation as children and find it difficult to form healthy relationships as adults also engage in sabotaging behavior toward others. This behavior, in turn, has the effect of worsening the condition of the insecure-anxious person, jeopardizing their career and their relationships with others, leading them further down the spiral of distress from which it sometimes seems difficult to escape.

## 2.4 The chains of codependency

Love is a very powerful emotion. When we meet someone who fits our ideal partner and is similar to what we seek, we feel a shift inside us. It may be the way he talks, the way he looks at us, or that irresistible smile. There is something about them that catches our attention beyond measure.

However, if you have been in a relationship for a moderate to long time, you will know that this "butterflies in the stomach" feeling does not last forever. The first few months are typically characterized by euphoria, uncertainty, and excitement, but in the following months, the relationship undergoes a change. Suddenly, you feel deep affection, a need for intimacy, and a desire for commitment. This is what marks the end of infatuation and the beginning of true love.

But these changes are not just a figment of our imagination. On a biological level, our organism also undergoes changes. The initial feeling of euphoria is caused by the pituitary gland receiving "arousal" stimuli from the hypothalamus, which is a brain structure that mediates between the nervous and hormonal systems. This structure also happens to be filled with the neurotransmitter of happiness, euphoria, and contentment: dopamine.

When the guy we like pays attention to us the first few times, compliments us, and calls us after the first date, the release of dopamine makes us feel like we're on a cloud. Of course, this emotional state cannot last forever. If established couples lived in a constant state of excitement and emotional arousal, it would take away their ability to live their daily lives with clarity, make well-considered decisions in various areas of life (including work), and maintain their relationship in a healthy and positive way. It doesn't happen because it's not evolutionarily wise; we need to be vigilant and rational in order to make really thoughtful decisions about everything.

So, what happens at a biological level? What causes this excitement and sense of adventure to diminish and instead increase the feeling of deep love that makes our partner a member of our family? It is attachment hormones, such as oxytocin and vasopressin, which are the same ones that create and strengthen the bond between a mother and her child.

However, it happens that some people never get past the initial phase of deep infatuation and enter the phase of deep love. The psychologist has given this intermediate state a precise name: "limerence" (Tennov, 1998).

Reading about the characteristics of limerence, I noticed many similarities with insecure-anxious attachment. In the list of limerence "symptoms," I found *intrusive thoughts about the partner, fear of rejection and abandonment, feelings of euphoria and contentment when the partner gives attention, constant and obsessive searching for signs of reciprocity from the partner, etc.* The list goes on, but I have also observed that limerence is similar to OCD, while anxious-insecure attachment seems to oscillate more between limerence and love.

That's right. If limerence does not depend on the partner's nature (loving or unloving, loving or absent), we have seen how in insecure-anxious attachment, the partner's inconsistency further exacerbates the compulsive nature (now referred to as limerence).

This confirms our earlier hypothesis that forming a relationship with a person of secure attachment can help break the chains of dependency, insecurity, and rumination. But what if this is harder than you think?

Although the following statement would make Bowlby and Ainsworth turn in their graves, it turns out to be truer than ever: the insecure-avoidant and the insecure-anxious are naturally attracted to each other like magnets! This is the most apt example of the saying, "opposites attract.".

We know very well that our conscious experience of life is not the only one we experience. There is an unconscious motive in everything we do, incomprehensible even to ourselves. Similarly, the insecure-anxious subject is attracted to the insecure-avoidant because it represents a kind of "challenge" or "prototype" of the person they would like to be. For example, if an insecure-anxious girl meets a mysterious boy, she may be attracted by the possibility of learning to be like him.

But this mutual attraction may also be caused by a confirmation and reinforcement dynamic. Indeed, the insecure-anxious may be attracted to the insecure-avoidant because the latter's behavior somehow confirms their belief that people disappoint and that the possibility of finding a secure base is only an illusion.

Similarly, the insecure-avoidant may be attracted to the insecure-anxious because the partner's obsessive behavior reinforces the insecure-avoidant's belief that they truly need independence and autonomy. For example, if an insecure-avoidant girl meets a jealous man who needs constant reassurance, she will tend to think, "Then I'm right to want to be on my own." And so, the vicious circle never ends.

And what about people who are securely attached? Since these people are generally able to recognize the characteristic of emotional unavailability in insecure-avoidants, they tend to reject them. This leaves the insecure-anxious looking for someone to love, and if they meet an insecure-avoidant, they may fall into a trap from which it will be difficult to get out.

So, if we started by talking about the insecure person's dependency on their partner, we can now talk about "codependency." Consider the case of my friend Ann. Have you ever wondered why Max didn't break up with her despite the fact that their relationship remained the same for three years? Or why he always maintained a minimum level of attention and affection so that Ann would always try to get close to him and not break up with him? Because, in reality, Max was just as dependent on Ann as she was on him.

I say "was" because their relationship ended several years ago. But I'll save those details for later when we uncover the story of Ann's therapy journey together. And no, I don't want to gossip, but I want to show you that there is a way out. The key is much closer than you think. In fact, it may already be in the palm of your hand.

# Chapter Three

# Us and Others

## 3.1 The Happiness Myth

"Try to focus on positive things and chase away negative thoughts!"

"Why are you always so sad? Cheer up, life is all about happiness!"

You must have heard these phrases a million times in your life. Whatever the form, tone, or intention, they all share the same basic assumption: being happy is normal and something we should all strive for.

We have all been brought up with the idea that happiness is the only emotion people should feel and that it is a "skill" to be learned over time. In short, everything must be done to achieve this state of *emotional perfection*. After all, if you were to ask your friends or acquaintances what they think the purpose of life is, I bet most of them would answer: "To be happy!"

So why is it so difficult? Are we the only ones who feel anxious when we argue with our partners? Couldn't we just relax? Well, no, it's not that simple. And if you feel abnormal, wrong, or strange when you suddenly experience negative emotions, there is a reason: our society lives on the false myth of happiness.

Russ Harris, a British doctor and psychotherapist, has written a successful book called *The Happiness Trap: Stop Struggling, Start Living*, in which he defends a thesis that seems to go against every foundation and ideal we have grown up with. He argues that happiness is only one of many emotions that human beings experience, and it is absolutely normal not to be happy all the time.

This philosophy is particularly important in our exploration of insecure-anxious attachment. If happiness is not the most normal emotion there is, it is only natural to feel pain, anxiety, and sadness when things do not go well.

But let's examine the basic points that Harris refutes in his book, which he refers to as "myths of happiness":

1. **"Happiness is the natural state of man."**

As we have briefly mentioned, we all grow up with the same false myth: happiness is the emotion we should all aim for. But where does this idea come from? More importantly, what does science have to say about it?

According to the World Health Organization, around 280 million people worldwide will suffer from some form of depression by 2023. So, if you're telling yourself that the whole world is happy and content except you, think again.

But it's not just about sadness. The study of human emotions began around 1960, when scientists Paul Ekman and Wallace V. Friesen identified the six main emotions: happiness, disgust, fear, sadness, surprise, and anger. They also studied all possible combinations of these emotions. A few years later, they even traveled to Papua New Guinea to see if there were any cultural differences. However, they concluded that regardless of ethnicity, religion, and culture, all people in the world experience the same six emotions (Ekman et al., 1987).

Since then, science has come a long way. While the spectrum of human emotions was previously thought to be limited to six, a recent study conducted in Berkley identified as many as 27 (Cowen & Keltner, 2017). Furthermore, another surprising finding revealed that many emotions do not represent a completely new state of mind. Instead, they exist as a middle ground between one emotion and another. For example, there is not only happiness but also adoration and wonder. There is not only fear but also horror, and so on.

In light of these arguments, and given the wide range of

emotions that human beings can experience, how can happiness be the most natural?

## 2. "If you are not happy, you are not normal."

The second myth of happiness somewhat represents Western society's view of what is normal and what is not. Many of us, when we feel sad for reasons that might seem silly to others, tend to judge ourselves in a negative way: *"If I feel angry about this event, there must be something wrong with me. It means I am not normal."*

This myth finds its most fertile ground in the universe of insecure-anxious attachment. Indeed, we have seen how the insecure-anxious person experiences feelings of pain, fear, and inferiority, which are often not understood or accepted by the partner.

In Ann's case, Max felt that Ann's feelings of frustration when he did not answer her phone were completely abnormal. This minimization, binomial happy = normal, sad = abnormal, tends to alienate the insecure-anxious person even more, making them feel even more misunderstood and believing they are what others see them as: outside the norm.

Once again, consider it from a more rational perspective: if humans have evolved to experience both negative and positive emotions, there is a reason for this. In fact, if you think about it, every negative emotion has a function.

For example, as we walk down a busy city street, emotions such as fear and surprise keep us on our toes in case a car fails to stop at the stop sign. At the same time, anger and sadness come to our aid, whispering in our ears, *"Hey, something is wrong here,"* to *warn us of harmful situations, events, or people.*

In the context of a dysfunctional relationship, is it distress, sadness, and fear that signal the presence of a problem and the need to resolve it?

For this reason, we are not abnormal when we experience all the whirlwind of emotions that others categorize as "negative"; it is simply our brain doing its arduous job of making us live life in all its facets.

3. **"To live well, we need to get rid of negative emotions."**

*"But how can I live a full life if all I feel is sadness?"*

You must have asked yourself this question a hundred times, perhaps after a fight with your partner or during moments of frustration or failure. ...Of course, the feeling of never being understood or of being judged does not help. And then you convince yourself: *"My life will be nothing but a succession of failures and defeats."*

But the idea that life should be all about happiness is just an illusion.

On a biological level, we humans, like our ancestors, are "designed" to cope with the challenges that life throws at us every day. Whereas a few millennia ago, it was all about finding food and escaping from predators, the advent of culture has changed the game. We no longer need to seek shelter in caves or build fires for warmth; culture and civilization have put it all within our reach. We may have houses, buildings, cars, jobs, and money that provide us with comfort, but even the modern individual has to "fight" every day. Whether it's a profession we've been working toward, the book we've been writing for years to be published, or whatever goal, big or small, we set ourselves from day to day, we all live for one purpose: personal fulfillment.

However, as you know, the road to any goal is often filled with obstacles. Before we achieve results, we're likely to make mistakes, which can trigger emotions other than happiness, such as disappointment, sadness, and even despair.

Consequently, the natural human condition is not a state of absolute happiness but a continuous alternation of contradictory and often negative emotions.

### 4. "We should all be able to control our emotions."

Undoubtedly, the myth of happiness makes us believe that we should not only strive for happiness but also aim to be in total control of ourselves and our emotions.

Think about the following question: How often have you seen your parents cry or express feelings of discomfort and frustration through words rather than actions? Chances are, very few times. This is because we humans are not used to expressing feelings other than joy and happiness.

Again, the relationship between Ann and Max is a good example. Because Ann was not encouraged by Max to express her feelings verbally, she had to resort to protest behavior to externalize what she was feeling, causing further damage to the relationship. But keeping everything inside not only damages our relationships with others, it also damages ourselves.

Excessive internalization of our emotions can worsen and transform the original feeling. Doubt can become anxiety, anxiety into fear, fear into anger, and so on.

But what happens when our emotions undergo these progressive transformations? Our body works a little like a pressure cooker: if we open the pot without letting the air out gradually, it will burst. In the same way, if we don't learn to recognize and express our emotions in a healthy and balanced way, we will end up feeling overwhelmed and confused.

At that point, it will be extremely difficult to control those emotions that even we no longer understand. The more we internalize a feeling, the more we move away from the matrix that created it. If you get into the habit of internalizing fear, you will find yourself experiencing panic attacks, which become more difficult to control.

In short, the last myth of happiness is debunked. As human beings, we must learn to express our feelings in a healthy way.

In this context, the insecure-anxious person is confronted with a particularly hostile context: they live in a society that demonizes them for the emotions they feel, making them feel wrong and alienated. It is no coincidence that several studies have found a strong association between insecure-anxious attachment and symptoms of generalized anxiety and depression (Jinyao et al., 2012).

But does all this suggest that we should give up on happiness? Absolutely not. In the words of Zygmunt Bauman, the famous Polish sociologist and author of many books, happiness is achieved by overcoming the difficulties that life presents us with every day.

It's not just about the myth of happiness. There are other factors that influence the mental health of insecure-anxious people. Let's find out together.

## 3.2 The role of social media

We are undeniably living in the age of social media. In the last twenty years, the world has undergone a revolution of sorts. Our parents had to use phone booths and landlines to make phone calls, while today, a simple message sent on WhatsApp is enough to reach someone within seconds.

This revolution does not stop at instant communication; social networks have broken down the barrier between private and public life. Think of the film stars of yesteryear: Audrey Hepburn, Marilyn Monroe, Marlon Brando... Who knows how they spent their days, what houses they lived in, what their favorite books were! In short, this bygone era retains a fascination of mystery that has been completely lost today.

But let's take it one step at a time. Today, everything is just a click away. If we used to live in doubt as to whether or not our partner was thinking of us, what they were doing, where they were, now things have changed. When Ann felt the need to be reassured, all she had to do was send a text message to Max, and if Max did not reply, his silence spoke louder than a thousand words. Given the immediacy of technology allowing us to stay connected at all times, his failure to reply increased Ann's distress.

**In this sense, the immediacy offered by social networks provides a kind of *positive feedback* to the anxiety of the insecure-anxious:**

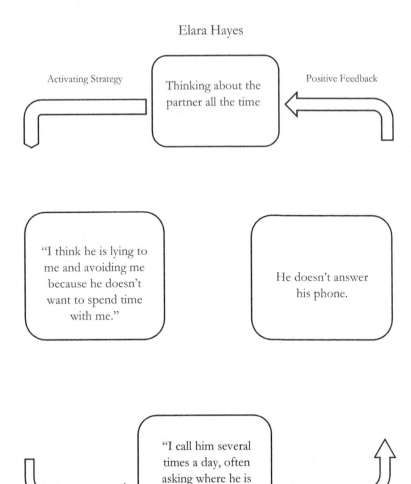

Positive feedback is nothing more than an event in reality, perceived or real, that confirms an individual's thoughts.

The affirmation "he's not answering the phone" confirms the insecure-anxious subject's activating strategy, which initiates the whole attachment system. When Ann became aware of the fact that Max was not answering the phone, her thoughts about him became even more obsessive, causing her to feed further doubts and beliefs that magnified this simple lack of response.

In general, positive feedback only feeds the pattern of anxious attachment, reinforcing the activating strategy and starting the loop again.

Are we saying that social media is the only positive feedback to the insecure-anxious loop? Absolutely not. This framework could be replaced by any other element that reinforces the individual's belief system. However, taking into account the current state of reality, it is undeniable that social media is an element that occupies a very influential position in everyday life.

Research has also found that insecure-anxious individuals have a special relationship with social media.

This study by Hart and colleagues (2015) looked at the behavior of 267 American participants between the ages of 19 and 73, examining their attachment style and relationship with Facebook.

The researchers found that those who exhibited symptoms of insecure-anxious attachment also showed obsessive behavior toward interactions on the platform. These people were more sensitive to the number of likes and comments they received from other users and generally spent more time online.

Since then, many more studies have been conducted on this topic, showing that the insecure-anxious are more likely to develop a full-blown addiction to social media (Chen et al., 2020) and to use social media as a means of satisfying their attachment needs (Stöven & Herzberg, 2021).

It seems that our current era is not conducive to the health of those with insecure-anxious attachments. But is it all about effective communication and positive feedback? Not really.

The advent of social networking in our everyday lives has also meant that we are constantly exposed to other people's lives. Just think of Instagram stories and how, with one click, we can take a peek at the lifestyles of celebrities and influencers, as well as regular people.

The fact that people can film 60 seconds of everyday moments (as with Instagram Stories) and present them to an audience as a sequence of events gives the impression that their lives consist only of these idyllic moments: living in dream homes, outings with friends, laughter, delicious food, and lots of fun. Inevitably, we all compare our "normal" lives with the seemingly "perfect" lives of others. As a result, the insecure-anxious person, already suffering from an inferiority complex, only suffers more, experiencing psychological and physical disorders that worsen their situation.

For example, a study published in *The Journal of Psychology* examined the relationship of insecure-anxious Greek students with their own bodies (Koskina & Giovazolias, 2010). The results showed that emotional dependency and fear of abandonment led both female and male participants to be self-conscious about their body image and to have weight-related concerns. They also showed that these feelings led to eating disorders, particularly in women.

In short, the overall picture is not a positive one. Of course, there is no doubt that social media has revolutionized the way we communicate, benefiting human relationships, the professional world, and many other areas.

However, at the same time, they have contributed to an even more hostile environment for that part of the population, estimated at around 20 percent, who have developed an insecure-anxious type of attachment. While they live in a world that labels them "strange" and "abnormal," it is this same system that enables them to sink further into their anxiety. How do you escape this trap, you may ask? The first step is to understand the individuals revolving around you.

# 3.3 Looking around

When I moved to Seattle after spending my entire youth in Maine, things were not immediately easy. As soon as I arrived in the big city, I realized that I would have to learn to fend for myself. I had to figure out how to navigate the traffic, make new friends, and set a new pace in my routine.

So, day after day, I started going to places that made me feel good: scientific conferences, art exhibitions, and cute cafes. Eventually, I made friends with some people who hung out in the same circles as me.

We all have specific needs and preferences. One way of feeling good in the world is to surround ourselves with people who love us and care for us. Similarly, in the previous chapters, we mentioned how a person with insecure-anxious attachment should try to relate to people with secure attachment and avoid the insecure-avoidant.

How can this be done? The first step, of course, is to know how to recognize them.

Let's start with the insecure-avoidant. This category of person is discussed extensively in this book. Broadly speaking, they are people who value personal independence, maintain distance (both emotional and physical), and are reluctant to commit fully.

However, is it fair to conclude that a person is avoidant just because they occasionally forget to answer their mobile phone? So, let's take a look at some other red flags to look out for, especially in the early days of dating.

Anxious avoiders tend to have *unrealistic ideas about love* and their ideal partner, which no one can live up to. Over time, because they have had unsatisfactory relationships, they have learned to categorize the characteristics of each ex as negative and as a symptom of people who are too clingy: demands for affection, reassurance, physical and emotional closeness, healthy communication, and an exchange of opinions with respect for the other person, etc.

And yet, as you can see, these are perfectly legitimate needs that any non-avoidant person has toward their partner. It follows that avoidants will always judge negatively any person who they feel is undermining their independence.

Avoidants are also known to *lack empathy* for others, even when it comes to their own partner. In a study conducted by Overall and colleagues (2015), insecure-avoidant individuals were videotaped having conversations with their partners and trying to get them to change their behavior.

The researchers then showed the video to the avoidants and analyzed their ability to detect a change in their partner's emotions. The results showed that although the avoidants were able to detect this change, they overestimated the intensity of the change toward the negative. For example, if the partner was disappointed, the avoidant would read anger or resentment in the partner's body language and facial expression. Furthermore, when the avoidant perceived an emotional change in their partner, they reacted with hostility and became defensive.

When I came across this study, I couldn't help but think back to Ann's words when talking about Max: *"... he never seems to understand how I feel, takes every little request I make (like maybe texting me when he goes out) as a restriction on his freedom and thinks I'm always nervous or angry!"*

What else? Avoidants also test or impose *small punishments*. If they think you don't understand or accept their way of being, they will make you pay for it. For example, if you call once too often during the period when they have asked you not to, they may resort to extreme measures such as blocking your calls or messages, causing your attachment system to skyrocket.

One of the "punishments" often inflicted by avoidants is *ghosting*, a practice that consists of disappearing, not answering for several hours or even days, and leaving the partner in a state of total confusion. When this happens, the insecure-anxious person's greatest fear suddenly takes shape in the thought: *"He has left me, just as I thought he would."*

Another typical avoidant behavior is *judging their partner negatively*, often comparing them to others, especially their ex. That's right, although the insecure-avoidant's previous partner was likely treated just as unkindly as their current one, they are magically seen in a new light once they become an ex. Suddenly, the avoidant realizes the mistake he made in letting them slip away.

When arguing with the current partner, it is not uncommon for the avoidant to use derogatory language toward them and celebratory language toward the ex: *"My ex wasn't as dramatic as you are"* or *"If only you were like my ex, we wouldn't have these problems."*

It follows that if the partner in question is insecure-avoidant, all these behaviors will only exacerbate the partner's sense of self-worth and insecurity. Given the characteristics of the insecure-avoidant outlined above, you might ask yourself: *"But how can they have satisfying relationships and make their partner happy?"* Answering this question would require another book, in which I would explain in detail the difficulties insecure-avoidants experience in their daily lives and give advice on how to overcome them.

However, it should be noted that even in their case, having a relationship with secure people is beneficial. They are able to recognize a basic difficulty in establishing intimacy without taking it personally. They are willing to communicate their needs effectively and teach their partner the basics of communication.

Now it's time to talk briefly about the secure attachment style— our needle in the haystack, our light at the end of the tunnel. How do you recognize these people out of a thousand?

As with avoidant and anxious people, it's not possible to recognize a secure person at a glance. You need to pay attention to how they react in certain situations.

To give an overview, I will quote below my observations on Ann's relationship with her new boyfriend, Paul, which I had written down in my notebook.

*Ann came out of her relationship with Max more shaken than ever. Although she found the strength to leave him, she is still convinced that part of the responsibility lies with her: maybe she was just too clingy. She has recently met another man, Paul, who doesn't seem to mind Ann's very expansive nature: he answers her phone calls enthusiastically, always tells her that he finds her unique and beautiful, and that what he loves most about her are her "flaws." But by flaws he means that she is a bit messy and that she can get lost in the streets, even with Google Maps under her eyes! Of being "clingy," "dramatic," or "exaggerated," not a shadow. When they argue, as all couples do, Paul is able to maintain a truly enviable calm: he tells Ann his impressions and opinions and then lets her explain hers... no argument has ever lasted more than half an hour... yet!*

When I met Ann again a few weeks later, I noticed a light in her that I thought had gone out forever. She seemed to have returned to the vibrant, confident, and enthusiastic girl I knew. But what had Paul done to bring her back to her old self?

First of all, as a proper secure, Paul understood the importance of emotional closeness and intimacy in a relationship. He believed in getting to know each other well, spending time together, and familiarizing themselves with each other's friends. He also accepted her insecurities as a normal characteristic of Ann, as of any human being. He knew that sometimes people look in the mirror and see themselves as ugly and undesirable, so he took it upon himself to remind Ann that she was special. Gradually, she began to see herself through his eyes and regained her self-esteem.

So, Ann's thought pattern gradually changed.

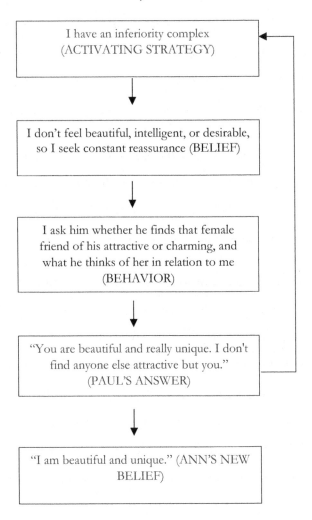

I have an inferiority complex
(ACTIVATING STRATEGY)

I don't feel beautiful, intelligent, or desirable,
so I seek constant reassurance (BELIEF)

I ask him whether he finds that female
friend of his attractive or charming, and
what he thinks of her in relation to me
(BEHAVIOR)

"You are beautiful and really unique. I don't
find anyone else attractive but you."
(PAUL'S ANSWER)

"I am beautiful and unique." (ANN'S NEW
BELIEF)

**Although everyone is different, here are Paul's general qualities to look for in the people you meet:**

- People who are comfortable with closeness and intimacy

- People who value you as a person and put you in a good light

- People who do not compare you with others, who celebrate your uniqueness with its virtues and faults

- People who do not run away from an argument but know how to handle it verbally and effectively

- People who reassure you when you doubt their love

- People who understand your sensitivity and do not blame you

If you look around and don't see anyone who can love you in this way, look again. Remember that if your past relationships have convinced you that you are not worthy of love, that you are wrong and abnormal, it only means that you have not yet found the right person.

# 3.4 Learn to know your triggers: a workbook

In the vast universe of psychology, the word "trigger" has a very important meaning. Throughout my years of research, I have come across this concept many times: an external element, a part of the environment that provokes an emotional response or makes us relive a past event.

To understand how this phenomenon works, we need only

think of the mechanism of Pavlovian conditioning. In the case of the dogs, the bell acted as a trigger, causing them to salivate. Although Pavlov deliberately "taught" his dogs this association in order to test its effects, more or less the same thing happens to us humans every day, but in an automatic way.

Let's explain this in more detail. From an evolutionary point of view, the organism of any living being is designed to respond efficiently to dangers in its environment. You may have heard of the fight-or-flight response, a physiological and psychological state of alertness that allows us to react or flee in the face of danger.

We humans share this ability with all animals in the world, of all species, and the reason is straightforward: this internal warning system is essential for survival. Imagine you are on safari in the African jungle. Suddenly, you see a lion in the distance. That's when your entire body activates to cope with the imminent danger: your blood flow, heart rate, and breathing rate increase to support your brain, which is working at breakneck speed; your muscles tense to prepare you for escape; and sweating increases.

At the same time, different parts of your brain communicate to prepare you for escape: the amygdala, responsible for the emotional response of fear, communicates with the prefrontal cortex to process this emotion rationally: "I'm afraid because I just saw a lion."

As you can see, this whole process is very similar to the physiological response to stress: sweating, accelerated heart rate, tense muscles, and so on. As you probably know, the physical sensation that follows a stressful episode is exhaustion. You may have experienced this after an activity that puts you under pressure, such as giving an important presentation at work or taking a difficult exam at university. This is because your body uses a lot of resources and energy to put you in the best possible condition to escape danger or to maintain your composure in a highly stressful situation.

At the same time, however, our brain is designed to minimize the amount of energy it uses and to function efficiently. In this context, the existence of "triggers" can be seen as a strategy used by the brain to conserve energy.

Imagine the following scenario: It's a gloomy day and you wake up in a bad mood. As you get ready to go to university or work, you send a good morning message to your partner, who does not reply. Your mood worsens and later that morning, your car decides to give you a hard time and refuses to start. When it finally does start, you find yourself stuck in a huge traffic jam. In the afternoon, you meet your partner for coffee and, because of your bad mood and partly his usual inconstancy, you argue and quarrel.

In this scenario, and during all the time you spent before the argument, your brain picked up elements here and there that made you uncomfortable, such as the rain, the unreturned message, the car not starting, and the early morning traffic. All these elements are what we call triggers that your brain uses to predict your vulnerability to further stress and, in this case, a possible fight with your boyfriend.

"What is the point?" you might ask. For example, if your brain recognizes rain as a stressful element, it will use it to warn you of a possible stress reaction later in the day. In short, your brain is saying to you: "Today, when it is raining and you are already in a bad mood, is not the day to have more stressful conversations with your boyfriend (about the quality of your relationship, your incompatibility, your neediness, and his aloofness), because you are already stressed and you will not be able to handle the conversation calmly!"

If you listen to this "sixth sense" and learn to recognize your triggers, you will save your organism a lot of energy. On the other hand, if you continue to expose yourself to further stress (the car that won't start, the traffic, the argument with your boyfriend), your organism will have to do its best to continue to function despite all these elements.

However, triggers are more personal and specific to each person and are not so easy to identify. In response to my example, you might say: "I didn't fight with my boyfriend because of the rain and my bad mood, but because he kept telling me I was wrong!" Of course, there are triggers of different kinds, such as those that make you more susceptible to stress (the rain, the traffic) and those that cause the fight itself (your boyfriend, who kept misunderstanding you during the fight).

**This is because triggers create a kind of "memory track" in your brain so that whenever a certain thing happens, a mechanism is triggered:**

Are you in a bad mood? Ding-dong: you are more prone to stress!

Does your boyfriend blame you? Ding-dong: you are about to fight!

With this in mind, being able to identify your triggers is key. Indeed, developing the ability to recognize alarm bells in our environment helps us to understand when it would be best to avoid exposing ourselves to further stress.

In the following chapters, we will take you step by step through some specific techniques to "desensitize" you to your triggers. Before we explore these techniques, here is a quick guide to how to start recognizing them.

1. Because the trigger causes a physiological and emotional stress response, paying attention to your body and noticing any changes is a good idea. Do you suddenly feel anxious, with a weight in your stomach and no idea why? Your body has probably picked up on various signals from your environment that are causing you stress.

2. Try to retrace the events of the day. The aim is not to avoid all stressful situations but to overcome them and manage them so that they become neutral and you can experience them naturally. To do this, it is important to start by focusing on individual elements. Perhaps the rainy day gives a gloomy atmosphere to your surroundings, but the real trigger was your partner's lack of response. How did that make you feel? Did it make you feel sad, frustrated... jealous? Try to focus on each emotion.

3. If you think you have correctly identified the matrix of your trigger, then a good solution is to address it. If the problem is your partner's lack of responsiveness, take a quiet moment together and try to talk to him about it. Talk about how his behavior makes you feel and try to ask him to change it. If, on the other hand, you feel inside that the real problem is not the unanswered message, and you continue to feel this pressing anxiety, then it is time to repeat the cycle by paying

attention to your physical changes and trying to identify the dominant emotion. Then, make a list of events and situations that make you feel this way.

Although this is a short guide, it is intended to introduce you to a very important practice that should become part of your daily routine: paying attention to your feelings and emotions, being able to name them without self-judgment, and going straight to the matrix, asking yourself: "What triggers this feeling in me?" "What can I do to change this feeling into another?"

Having reached this point, Chapter Four will be entirely dedicated to discussing the best practices for taking care of yourself deep inside, such as resilience, compassion, and acceptance of vulnerability. Remember, to be able to love others and be loved, it is essential to be able to love yourself first.

# Chapter Four

# Navigating Your Emotions and Inner Self

## 4.1 What is emotional intelligence?

Many of us, myself included, grow up with an often mistaken idea of what intelligence is. In fact, this mental ability is usually associated with good academic performance, especially in science and math. Remember when you were a child and came home from school with a good grade on your math test and felt proud of your brilliance?

The idea that good school grades are a measure of intelligence is not entirely wrong. In fact, when the first IQ test was invented in 1912, it was thought that this was the only kind of intelligence that existed. But things soon changed. Shortly afterward, Daniel Goleman, an American psychologist, introduced the concept of emotional intelligence. The fact that you may not excel in science does not necessarily mean you are incompetent in all other areas of life.

Subsequently, other types of intelligence were introduced: the ability to get a good grade on a math test fell under the category of logical-mathematical intelligence, the ability to learn several languages easily under the category of linguistic intelligence, and so forth.

As you can imagine, the type of intelligence we are interested in for the purposes of this book is neither mathematical nor linguistic nor artistic. Instead, we are going to focus specifically on emotional intelligence.

What is emotional intelligence? To quote Goldman, it refers to *"abilities such as being able to motivate oneself and persist in the face of frustrations; to control impulse and delay gratification; to regulate one's moods and keep distress from swamping the ability to think; to empathize and to hope"* (Goleman, 1995).

One of the main reasons why we may not have great emotional intelligence, such as not excelling in some or all of the points above, is that no one has ever taught us. In fact, emotional intelligence is a skill that can be learned, just like reading, writing, or riding a bike.

To be more specific, Goldman believes that there are different types of emotional intelligence, and most of the emotional intelligence training that exists in the world has been developed around this model.

## 1. Being able to recognize your own emotions

The first fundamental step is to learn to recognize our emotions by being able to distinguish pain from anger and frustration from sadness. Did you know that this capacity also affects our ability to make rational decisions? If you can understand that the emotion you are feeling is sadness rather than anger, you will avoid making hasty decisions dictated by impulsiveness.

But is there a specific technique that can be used to distinguish one emotion from another?

In this regard, a team of researchers from Aalto University conducted a very interesting study (Nummenmaa et al., 2014). They tested a group of 700 participants from both Western and Eastern countries (to rule out a cultural component associated with the perceived emotion) and showed them scenes from films or excerpts from stories. They then asked them to indicate on a body map where they felt a particular emotion.

Incredibly, from the responses of 700 participants, the researchers were able to create a map of the human body based on the emotions felt. Anger, for example, seems to produce a strong sensation in the fists and head, while fear produces a kind of pressure on the chest. Shame, on the other hand, seems to almost inflame the cheeks, while love and happiness seem to "light up" the whole body.

The next time you are unsure about what kind of emotion you are feeling, try to refer to this table and identify the part of the body that you feel is "on fire." This will make it easier for you to distinguish one emotion from the other.

| | |
|---|---|
| **Anger** | Strong heat sensation to chest, fists, and head |
| **Fear** | Heat sensation from head to lower abdomen, with focus in center of chest |
| **Disgust** | Heat sensation from head to lower abdomen, with a focus on mouth and throat |
| **Happiness** | Feeling of warmth throughout the body, from head to toe, with a focus on the head, center of the chest and wrists |
| **Sadness** | Burning sensation in the eyes and mouth and in the middle of the chest; cold sensation in the rest of the body |
| **Surprise** | Burning sensation in the chest and head, heat in the eyes, and cold sensation in the legs |
| **Anxiety** | Heat sensation in the center of the chest, burning sensation in the head, neck, and lower abdomen; cold |

| | |
|---|---|
| | sensation in the legs |
| **Love** | Heat sensation in the head, chest, and lower abdomen; burning sensation in the arms and thighs |
| **Depression** | Cold sensation throughout the body |
| **Shame** | Heat sensation in the cheeks; burning sensation in the head, chest, and stomach; cold sensation in the arms and legs |

*Adapted from "Bodily Maps of Emotions," by Nummenmaa, L., 2014, Proceedings of the National Academy of Sciences of the United States of America, 111, p.647. Copyright 214 by PNAS.*

## 2. Being able to regulate your emotions

At this point, remembering the previous chapter, you might say, *"What about the talk about the myth of happiness and not always having to control your emotions?"* You are right, but emotional intelligence is not about control; it is about *modulation*. In relation to the myth of happiness, we discussed how important it is not to internalize an emotion but to be able to express it in the right way. Let's see how.

Two of the most effective techniques for learning to regulate your emotions are mindfulness and sensorimotor psychotherapy. These techniques work together with the following logic: if it's difficult to control emotions and bodily states through reasoning and thinking (top-down process), then one must learn to control the mind through the body (bottom-up process).

The main purpose of mindfulness is to make you aware of the *here* and *now*, all the sensations that are part of your being, and above all, to welcome them without any form of judgment (hence the absence of reasoning).

One of the most important resources and techniques for perceiving the here and now is *grounding*, also known as movement resource. To practice grounding, take a comfortable position on the floor, possibly cross-legged. With your eyes closed, focus solely on perceiving your feet and pelvis on the floor, feeling the support that the earth beneath your body provides. You are here (in this physical place) and now (in the present).

Then, let's talk about the *breath*, which is considered to be a somatic resource. It's one of the most powerful resources for exercising control over your mind. Assume a comfortable posture and try to focus solely on your breath. Try to imagine the path your breath takes from the moment it enters your nostrils until it reaches your lungs and exits again.

The act of breathing is one of the reflexes that our body performs automatically to keep us alive. However, we are not aware of this, not only because it is automatic, but because our mind keeps us constantly "busy" with thoughts. Human beings can never stop thinking. We can never "turn off" that little inner voice that guides our actions. Therefore, we must learn to stop thinking and concentrate on a physiological action that also controls the expression of emotions.

For example, think about how the emotion of anger or fear is expressed. Does it not seem to you that your heart begins to beat fast, almost wildly? This is nothing more than oxygen. If you reduce the amount of oxygen reaching your organs by controlling your breathing, then your body cannot physically produce the flight-or-fight response that we spoke about earlier.

What does all this mean? That if you learn to regulate your breathing and focus on the here and now, you will always be able to regulate and control your emotions and avoid exploding like a pressure cooker.

3. **Knowing how to read other people's emotions**

This ability is also known as empathy, the capacity to put yourself in another person's shoes and feel what they are feeling. You might wonder: *"But if I can barely recognize my own emotions, how can I possibly recognize those of others?"* There is some truth in this observation. Empathy, like many other resources of emotional intelligence, is a skill that can be learned.

However, humans, like other creatures, are endowed with a specific brain mechanism that enables them to interact with others in a profound way. In 1996, a group of researchers at the University of Parma carried out a study that changed our understanding of how some creatures interact. In a group of macaques, they identified a category of cells that they later called "mirror neurons": these cells were activated both when the monkey performed an action and when the monkey saw the researcher perform the same action (Gallese et al., 1996).

While we might find it difficult to empathize with others, our organism is designed to understand the intentions of others, their motivations, and their actions. When our partner or a friend is experiencing emotional pain or extreme happiness, we have all the prerequisites to put ourselves in their shoes and connect with them in a profound way.

Clearly, understanding the emotions we feel is fundamental to recognizing the same emotions in others. But if we can learn to locate an emotion in our body and through mirror neurons, we should also be able to perceive the same emotion in others. What is the element that blocks this understanding that makes some people less empathetic than others? That's right: *language.* We may be able to feel an emotion and perceive it in others, but we may not be able to name it and process it.

Indeed, Izard and colleagues (2011) discuss how the correct development of language in children facilitates their ability to understand the emotions of others. We can think of the human brain as a kind of black and white drawing. At birth, we all have the same brain structures, the same neurons, and the same learning capacity (the lines of the drawing). As we grow up, colors, shades, perspectives, and depths are added to the same drawing. In the same way, synaptic connections are made in our brains, memory is born, and we acquire the ability to attach meaning to events and places, including through the use of language.

And what better way to expand your vocabulary and language than through reading? In this respect, try to find some time for yourself, choose your favorite books, and start reading. This way, you will feed your imagination and also enhance your ability to understand others in depth and even help them understand themselves better.

## 4.2 From anxious to secure

In the previous chapters, we discussed the importance of surrounding oneself with people who have secure attachments so that the insecure-anxious person's mental schema does not become a dysfunctional mechanism that reinforces their anxiety. If the insecure-anxious person enters into a relationship with an avoidant person, the avoidant person will not be able to calm the insecure-anxious person's attachment system.

On the other hand, if the insecure-anxious person enters into a relationship with a secure person, the latter will be able to break the chains that keep the insecure-anxious individual in the trap of their own anxiety.

It's not wise, however, to base one's well-being entirely on the possibility of meeting a secure person. No matter who is around us, we all need to equip ourselves with the resources to be well on our own. Simply put, when everything around us is falling apart, we need to build a solid base to keep us afloat.

In this way, if we are not fortunate enough to encounter a secure partner who can help change our mental patterns, we must learn to do it ourselves or seek help through psychotherapy.

Cognitive Behavioral Therapy (CBT), which emerged in the last years of the last century, is based on this general assumption:

**If we change the way we think, our emotions will change and so will our behavior.**

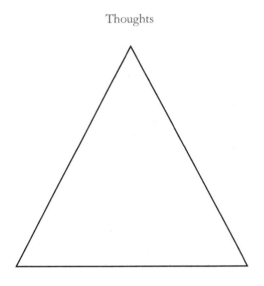

Thoughts

Actions                                              Feelings

In a nutshell, the therapist *cognitively restructures* the patient, and this can be done in a number of ways.

In fact, CBT is not a technique in itself, but a school of thought. It has branched out into different applications and techniques. One of these is the *logical-empirical style*, which is based on the practice of questioning the patient's thinking, refuting their beliefs by dismantling their logic.

Returning to Ann's example, you may recall that she did not change her attachment style through the influence of a secure partner. On the contrary, Ann went to therapy precisely to find the strength to leave Max, her former insecure-avoidant ex. It was only later that Ann met Paul and recognized in him the great value of his secure attachment style.

**Here is a typical conversation that Ann had with her psychotherapist (T), based on the logical-empirical style of CBT:**

*T:* *So, when you think about your relationship with Max, what is your biggest fear?*

*A:* *My greatest fear? Well... I have many.*

*T:* *All right. But I'd like you to try and identify the one you fear the most. Can you try?*

*A:* *Then I'd say that I'm afraid he won't love me anymore. That from one day to the next he will stop loving me and disappear into thin air.*

*T:* *Good. And if you think this will happen, how do you imagine it?*

*A:* *Well... I think it could happen if we fight. He doesn't like fighting; he always says it's stupid and useless. Then, he goes for a walk or disappears for a few hours. For me it's important to talk, so I call him, send him messages, ask him to meet and talk. But he doesn't answer for a couple of hours.*

*T:* *In these cases, do you fear that he will never answer again and disappear?*

*A:* *Yes, sometimes I think so. I mean, if he can't handle small arguments, how can I expect him to tell me when he decides to leave me? He seems incapable of any kind of discourse!*

**T:** *I see. But thinking about it, what are the chances, from 1 to 10, that Max will actually leave you?*

**A:** *I'd say an 8.*

**T:** *An 8? And on what evidence do you base this assessment?*

**A:** *I guess... on my personal thinking. On my fear that it will happen.*

**T:** *On your fear... but apart from your fear, what do you base this rating on?*

**A:** *I think just on that. I mean, no proof that he wants to do it. He has never done it and he has never told me that he wants to do it. That's my impression....*

**T:** *Okay. Now that you have established that it is your impression, would you reassess that probability?*

**A:** *I think so... I would give it a 5.*

Here is a practical example of what it means to do cognitive restructuring. What can we learn from this conversation? First, the therapist never suggests answers for Ann but asks the right questions. It was Ann who realized that the possibility of Max leaving her was based on her own impression and fear, not external evidence. While Max did not engage in a discourse, he responded to Ann's needs with silence. However, he didn't threaten to leave her, and he didn't tell her that he didn't love her anymore....

Through this technique, the therapist also teaches the patient to think critically about their fears, doubts, and insecurities. The aim is not to convince the patient that a thought is wrong but to give them a basis for evaluating its meaningfulness and truthfulness.

Initially, Ann's mental schema triangle looked something like this.

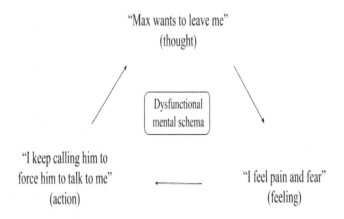

"Max wants to leave me"
(thought)

Dysfunctional
mental schema

"I keep calling him to
force him to talk to me"
(action)

"I feel pain and fear"
(feeling)

After many sessions of logical-empirical cognitive restructuring, Ann's pattern was modified in this way.

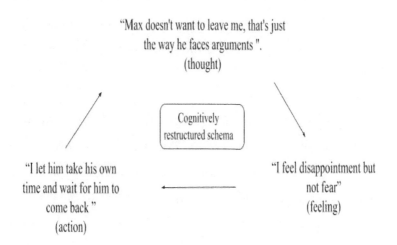

Of course, cognitive restructuring does not happen in a single dialogue. Sometimes it takes months, if not years, for the therapist to completely change the patient's mental pattern so that emotions and actions also benefit.

So, it can be quite difficult to embark on this journey alone, without the help of a specialist therapist. However, there are some small techniques and tricks to help you change the way you think.

For example, now that you know that it is possible to change your thinking, try questioning your beliefs, just as a psychotherapist would. Try writing the following questions in a notebook and answering them when you feel a pressing thought or one of the activating strategies.

1.  What frightens you?

2.  Why does it frighten you?

3.  On a scale of 1 to 10, how likely is it that your fear will come true?

4.  Is it as bad as you think? If so, why?

5.  Are there any other possible outcomes?

6.  If yes, what is the most likely outcome?

The act of writing down your thoughts and seeing them change as a result of these questions has a very specific purpose: the next time you feel that another dysfunctional thought is getting the better of you, retrace the path of your answers to the previous doubts and use the same method again.

Over time, you will notice small changes. For example, the very act of stopping, picking up the notebook, and writing is what stands between the dysfunctional thought and the action. If, after the thought, *"He has high standards of beauty and intelligence that I will certainly not reach (belief),"* you make an effort to pause and refute this belief, you will not jump to the usual hasty conclusion: *"I need constant reassurance and I ask him if he finds his friend attractive (behavior or protest behavior)."*

This process will certainly lead you to different conclusions. In this case, unless you have evidence that your partner might find another girl attractive (he has flirted with someone in the past, neglected you in favor of his "friend," etc.), you will certainly realize that your fear is either irrational or stems from an experience with a previous partner.

Generally speaking, this exercise introduces your brain to a different, more critical way of thinking. Suddenly, you are no longer alone with your fear, but you have a few aces up your sleeve, such as mental flexibility, the ability to reason, and an inner strength you had not yet discovered.

## 4.3 Facing fears head-on

Remember the section where we talked about the myth of happiness and how it can exacerbate the condition of the anxious-insecure? Russ Harris, author of *The Happiness Trap: Stop Struggling, Start Living*, not only listed the problems of our society but also approached the subject from a clinical point of view.

**The solutions he proposes are based entirely on Acceptance and Commitment Therapy (ACT), a cognitive behavioral therapy that focuses on two fundamental elements:**

- Acceptance: learning to accept every feeling and emotion, as mindfulness teaches us

- Motivation: learning to proactively pursue personal goals.

In short, it's the combination of these two skills (acceptance and motivation) that helps us turn our attention away from past events that have generated past emotions (fear of abandonment, uncertainty, doubt) and focus on the present without self-judgment. In addition, the motivation component ensures that this change in mindset is sustained over time.

Since its theoretical inception in 2004 (Hayes), ACT has been shown to be an effective technique for treating anxiety and depression, chronic pain, emotional addictions, and relationship problems. For example, this type of therapy can be particularly useful in dealing with the problem of insecure-anxious attachment.

**Like all psychological techniques, ACT is based on a philosophical principle. In this case, the principle is called *Relational Frame Theory*, which supports the following points:**

- Throughout our lives, we have learned to relate events through language, and this is also why we learn language (e.g., *I say to myself, "When I asked my mother for help, she was never available"*).

- Psychological pain results from people trying to solve

"dilemmas" belonging to the external world (any external obstacle that requires problem-solving skills) through the internal structures created by language.

Sounds like a lot of words, doesn't it? It is actually quite simple. The basic assumption is this: inner suffering is a normal state, as is sadness and all other emotions (just as we said when we talked about happiness). However, we need to distinguish between suffering and pain. Pain and mental pathologies arise when we try to solve dilemmas and problems through mental schemas that we might call dysfunctional (born through language).

It is a bit like applying the original thought to any area of life: *"My mother never helped me in the past when I asked her to."* If we relate to a person, partner, or friend with the same thought (expressed linguistically by this phrase), we fall victim to insecure-anxious attachment: *"Just as my mother did not help me in the past, my partner will not help me either."*

In fact, a fundamental point of ACT is the focus on the present: if an event happened in the past, it does not mean that it will happen again in the future. Similarly, if one person has behaved in a certain way, it does not mean that all people will behave in the same way.

What is the difference between a purely cognitive behavioral approach and ACT?

In a cognitive behavioral approach, you focus on the symptom, such as heart palpitations in the case of anxiety or tension in the case of fear. The aim is to change the mental pattern to change the symptom. Consider the technique of *systematic desensitization*, which involves exposing the patient to the anxiogenic object (perhaps a situation that causes jealousy in the patient, if jealousy is the problem) and then inducing a relaxation stimulus in the patient to counteract their natural fear response.

In the case of ACT, the approach is quite different. According to this model, symptoms are understood as *values*, meaning they indicate the individual's deepest desires, which they would like to pursue. In this sense, symptoms/values are not to be "solved" or eliminated. On the contrary, a strategy must be implemented to help us pursue these values in a healthy way.

Let's take an example. When Ann approached her therapist, one of the symptoms she presented was severe anxiety. In ACT, one of the first therapeutic steps is acceptance. It was important for Ann to understand that she was anxious. It was not anger, frustration, or sadness. When you notice that you are feeling a certain way, the natural human instinct is to judge the emotion and judge yourself: *"Of course, I'm worried because Max thinks my worries are stupid, he doesn't reassure me in any way, and he ignores me…"* Sure. However, ACT teaches us to refrain from any judgment, to accept the emotion, and observe it with curiosity in relation to the present.

We must observe the emotion of fear, befriend it, and ask it: *"What do you want? Why do you exist?"* Remember that symptoms are values and deep desires. In Ann's case, her deep desire was not for reassurance (as she claimed), for Max to answer her call, or for her to stop feeling jealous. What Ann wanted, deep in her heart, was to feel loved at last. Only then would she be able to shine in the other areas of her life, to develop her career, to nurture her friendships. The problem was not a mobile phone call, but a deep need for love.

Slowly, Ann realized she was looking for love and happiness in the wrong place and with the wrong person. Of course, through several sessions of cognitive restructuring, she learned to give events their proper weight: *"If Max doesn't answer my calls, it doesn't mean he's cheating on me,"* or *"If he wants to spend time alone, it doesn't mean he's bored with me."* However, she also realized she could never be happy with Max in the sense that she intended. Regardless of her (counterproductive) attempts, Max would always put his independence, free time, and inner peace first. This realization began Ann's journey of acceptance and also identifying and pursuing her own goals.

In this chapter, we have introduced psychological techniques that can be useful in managing and possibly resolving some aspects of insecure attachment. However, finding a secure attachment partner will not guarantee a problem-free relationship. Remember, all couples experience difficulties at some point. For this reason, the next chapter will look in detail at some of the basic issues you need to consider when you are with someone, as well as offering specific exercises to improve your relationship with yourself and your life as a couple.

# Chapter Five

# Pathways to Overcoming Anxious Attachment

## 5.1 What is the role of evolution?

Throughout this book, we have talked about development, evolution, behavior, and genetic inheritance. We have also discovered how the advent of science and culture has allowed us to study the human mind and understand that altering the way we think means changing the way we act.

Just as almost everything in nature has a purpose, different types of attachment have a purpose in evolution too.

Many animal species, including humans, have won the battle against extinction thanks to a trump card that not all living beings have: cooperation. Just think of how modern society works: individuals form families, work in groups, and socialize. Similarly, around 300,000 years ago, Homo sapiens understood a fundamental concept: if you cooperate, your chances of survival increase.

While the male went out hunting to provide food for himself and his family, the female took care of her offspring. This structure may seem obvious to us, as it has continued down to the present day (and is still the predominant structure in many parts of the world). This division of labor has made a real difference in the dominance of Homo sapiens over all other species. Suffice it to say that orangutans behave differently. The male leaves the female immediately after mating and does not contribute to the rearing of offspring.

So, humans have a few tricks up their sleeve that have allowed their species to thrive. In addition to cooperation, another trump card is diversity. Humans, like many other species, have evolved in a thousand different ways. This allows for at least some of the species to survive unfavorable conditions and not face extinction.

But what does all this have to do with our discussion of insecure-anxious attachment? Incredibly, even the three main styles have an evolutionary component that you wouldn't expect.

Let's start with secure attachment. Although the concept of monogamy didn't exist at the time of Homo sapiens, the predominance of the family and its structure suggested the existence of a secure attachment. As we have said, parents worked together to bring up their children and shared responsibilities between them. More recently, 20,000 years ago, monogamy was born. According to some experts, Neanderthals no longer felt the need to mate with as many females as possible. Did they perhaps realize that taking care of a single-family unit improved their chances of succession? After all, it's not enough to bring children into the world; you also have to take care of them.

But if this family structure seems ideal, why did the other types of relationships emerge? Have they upset some kind of balance? In evolutionary terms, there is always a reason.

Think of butterflies: some of them evolved into moths two centuries ago to camouflage themselves on soot-covered tree trunks in the most polluted parts of the world, including the UK. Similarly, a group of humans realized that an exclusively secure bond was not fully beneficial to their chances of survival. Perhaps, at some point in history, humans developed the ability to fend for themselves? To learn to rely on themselves? This would explain the emergence of insecure-avoidant attachment. Then, when we felt in danger and vulnerable, insecure-anxious attachment might have allowed the individual to attach to a source of protection in an attempt not to be alone.

What we are sure of, however, is that these "character traits" have survived to the present day and that natural selection has allowed them to persist (Ein-Dor et al., 2010).

However, the struggle for survival today is different from the past. The sole purpose of relationships is not limited to the succession of genes but has expanded to include stability, security, mutual trust, satisfaction, and happiness in a romantic relationship. As our expectations and needs have changed, so has the nature of the bond we should form with our other half.

Knowing the mechanisms that govern and guide us is always the first step toward change. It's not only me who says this but also Carl Jung: *"Until you make the unconscious conscious, it will run your life and you will call it fate."* In a nutshell, he explains that unless we understand the mechanisms of our unconscious (what we are not fully aware of), we will attribute everything that happens around us to fate, to the natural flow of events. Consequently, if we believe that we are not responsible for what happens in our lives, we will not even try to make changes.

For a happy and satisfying relationship, secure attachment is just the foundation on which we can build a great castle. What are the other skills we need to develop in a relationship?

Let's look at them together.

## 5.2 Setting boundaries

When you embark on a path of psychotherapy or personal

growth, you are usually dealing with a specific individual: yourself. You talk to the therapist, you do exercises on yourself, you try to improve yourself, but you have to remember that when you are in a relationship, you are not alone—there are two people involved. To build a healthy relationship, you need to work on it with your partner, communicate your needs, and meet each other's expectations. One of the basic skills to develop is to set limits, set stakes, and not cross them.

You see, in romantic relationships, as in friendships, it's important to know how to respect each other, which requires communicating your expectations from the start. However, people often are unaware of their own inner workings. Ann, for example, didn't know what she was getting into when she started a relationship with Max. She had never experienced such intense jealousy before him, and she had never been a particularly insecure girl. So, when she was confronted with Max for the first time, she couldn't quite define her unknown whirlwind of emotions.

The advantage of having different experiences and testing yourself is that you learn insights about yourself that you didn't know before. When this happens, it's good to share these little discoveries with those around you, especially with your significant other.

For example, after her psychotherapy sessions, Ann learned to share different aspects of her personality with Paul once they started dating seriously.

*"You know, over the last few years, I have discovered that I am a very affectionate person. That's why I like to spend a lot of time with the person I'm dating, to be involved in their life and I don't like it when they disappear for hours on end without saying anything. What do you think?"*

Of course, Ann developed this knowledge after a lot of work on herself. But what can you do if you are not sure what your limits and preferences are or what causes you pain and distress? A good method is role-playing, both to get to know yourself better and to make yourself known to your partner.

What is role-playing? It's an exercise in which you set up hypothetical situations and ask yourself: *"What would I do in this situation?" "How would I react?" "How would I feel in a similar context?"* If you already know your own attachment style, this exercise can also help you get to know your partner's attachment style better.

Here are some hypothetical scenarios you could suggest.

1. *"Imagine you are at your parents' house in your hometown for the summer holidays and I am not there. One evening you go out and meet a group of old friends, including your ex. You all sit down for a drink and tell each other about your lives. How would you deal with your ex in relation to me?"*

Usually, an insecure-avoidant doesn't believe that their behavior in certain situations can affect their partner's feelings. In general, they don't like to feel responsible for other people's feelings. In the carefree and detached way that characterizes them, an avoidant might reply: *"I don't think I'd do anything special; I'd just talk to my ex in a normal way."* In contrast, a person with a secure attachment might be more aware of their own actions and, in particular, how to approach the insecure-anxious partner. So, they might say something like: *"I would probably call or text you, make you aware of the situation, and ask you if my ex's presence makes you feel uncomfortable."*

There's no right or wrong answer in these scenarios, but they can still give you an idea of how someone thinks, deals with situations, and relates to you.

Another typical situation might be:

2. *"Imagine that you and I have planned a holiday abroad with friends. The night before, I get a bad fever and have to cancel my reservation. What would you do?"*

Given the individualistic style of an insecure-avoidant, they would probably go anyway. Of course, they would be sorry about your fever and your need to stay at home, but they wouldn't think it was any of their business. After all, they have already booked their flight and hotel and would lose a lot of money! On the contrary, a secure person would immediately be more concerned about your feelings and would almost certainly decide not to go.

**Here's one last scenario you could suggest before you draw any conclusions about who you're with:**

3. *"Imagine you are with me at an exhibition, perhaps organized by a friend of yours. I don't know your friends very well and you are introducing me to some of them at this event. At some point I say or do something that upsets you. Think of something that might upset you that I am not aware of. What would you do?"*

When faced with a similar situation, the insecure-avoidant might tell you off explicitly: they may sulk, ignore you in front of others, or correct you in front of others. Whatever the situation, the important thing is that you learn your lesson. In contrast, a partner with a secure attachment would take into account the context, your insecurity, and your naivety. With this in mind, they would wait until the two of you are alone to make you aware of your mistake and talk about it calmly.

**Using these three scenarios, we again compared the behavior of an insecure-avoidant and a secure person. This time, however, we did so on three different levels:**

1. Their concern for your feelings, also known as "empathy"

2. Their tendency to care for you in times of need

3. Their way of dealing with emotions and assessing context

By testing the ground through hypothetical scenarios, you can predict certain outcomes that go beyond the hypothetical scenario. For example, if your partner didn't take your feelings into account when they met their ex, they would probably react with the same indifference to other situations that make you feel anxious and uncomfortable. Similarly, if they told you that they would still go on holiday if you were ill at home, they would probably not be the right person to call in an emergency. And so on.

Again, framing your partner through fictional situations, rather than when the drama really happens, allows you to make your point and avoid being confronted with real and uncomfortable events.

For example, you could explain to your partner that you can be insecure at times. So, when they sit at the table with their ex, you could tell them that you would prefer them to put you at ease and be interested in your point of view. Once you have challenged their point of view, you also have a chance to explore how willing they are to come to you. Do they stick to their guns? Do they agree with you? Testing their negotiation skills will also give you an idea of how they approach arguments. Are they always on the defensive, or do they seem reasonable and understanding?

Remember that getting to know yourself and others is not a quick or easy process. Sometimes it takes patience. But with a little imagination, you can explore your own boundaries and discover feelings and limitations that you never knew existed.

## 5.3 The trust factor

Have you ever baked a cake? Or at least know something about the world of pastry? You don't have to be a professional pastry chef to know that, unlike cooking, pastry requires a perfect balance of proportions, quantities, and ingredients. For example, while it doesn't matter how many beans you use to make a full English breakfast, or whether you poach or scramble your eggs, things change when you make pudding: the amount of butter, sugar, and eggs really does make a difference.

What has this got to do with our book? It's nothing more than a metaphor. In romantic relationships, as in desserts, there are those elements that are fundamental and hold the various ingredients/pieces together perfectly: understanding, communication, empathy, loyalty, friendship, respect, support, and trust.

There is no such thing as "a bit of trust" or "a pinch of loyalty."

No, these components are fundamental and must be included in their entirety.

Among these ingredients, there is one that some would argue is almost the most important of all in romantic relationships. It's like flour for English muffins—without it, all the other ingredients would fall apart. This ingredient acts as a kind of glue. In relationships, that ingredient is **trust**.

It's not just trust in the sense of loyalty (the two are different). Trust is all those actions and behaviors that give you confidence that your partner is someone you can count on. Can you call them in a time of need? Can you tell them a secret? Can you count on them for practical support and to be on your side in a conflict with others? And so on.

Trust is also a value that varies from country to country, from culture to culture. For example, a recent survey found that the countries where people trust each other the most are China and India, while in countries such as Turkey, Brazil, and Malaysia, people tend to be more suspicious (Jackson, 2022). So, is it a cultural issue? Surely, the question is more complicated. Economic, social, political, and many other factors come into play.

One of the leading researchers in the field of relationships is John Gottman, an American psychologist and professor.

Throughout his career, Gottman has tried to "quantify" the concept of trust by defining and explaining what it really is. So, he took couples and asked them to have a conversation while being filmed. He then had them watch the same footage and asked them to rate the conversation according to their personal opinion, simply to determine how they thought the conversation was going.

The results gave Gottman a lot to think about. In fact, it turned out that each participant thought the conversation was going well when they were getting the better of the other. And these results held true for most of the participants. What does all this mean? This suggests that many couples see their relationship and their communication as a kind of competition in which they have to outdo each other. Gottman called this phenomenon "the metric of betrayal," where one person "wins" (a conversation) only by defeating a partner. In this verbal exchange, the members of a couple seem to become rivals who "betray" each other every second.

What about cooperation? The teamwork with which a couple should build their relationship? That's right: as a couple, you should be happy about each other's successes, encourage each other, and not see each other as eternal rivals. And the worst part is that many of us score high on the metric of betrayal (competing with our partner) without even realizing it.

Gottman shared an episode from his married life that perfectly illustrates the concept of trust in its broadest sense. One evening, after returning home from work, he was about to read the last pages of a book he had been meaning to finish. He found himself lying on his bed, relaxed, with the book in his hand. He 'couldn't wait to plunge back into the story and discover the ending! Suddenly, he saw the image of his wife in the mirror, with a sad expression on her face. Standing there in front of the mirror, she looks like someone who could really use a big hug. At that moment, Gottman had to make a choice: pretend he didn't see his wife and continue reading the book or put his wife's well-being ahead of his own pleasure and desire. As a good psychologist and husband, Gottman chose to close the book and comfort his wife, ask her what was wrong, and offer his support. This is a perfect example of what the word trust means in a relationship.

Gottman didn't just speculate on the issue of trust and its absence in romantic relationships; he offered solutions. In fact, according to him, trust is a skill that can be developed and built, which is how the *Gottman Trust Revival Method* was born. Let's see what it's all about.

This method is particularly useful for rebuilding trust after a betrayal, but it can also be used when trust in a relationship has faltered for other reasons. Perhaps the partner has lied or failed to offer support in times of need. First of all, the betrayed partner should examine their own conscience and ask themselves: *"Do I still value my partner despite the betrayal I have suffered?" "Do I feel such anger or resentment that it prevents me from affectionately caring for my partner?"* In short, it's necessary to ask oneself about the concrete possibilities of getting back together and being able to love each other without anger or resentment. If you decide to forgive someone, you must do it completely and avoid holding past mistakes against them.

**Once these internal conflicts have been resolved, you can proceed to apply the three steps of Gottman's Method:**

### 1. Atone

At this early stage, it's important that the cheating partner takes all the blame for the betrayal. When accused of any wrongdoing, cheating, or otherwise, there is usually a tendency to blame others. *"I cheated because I often felt ignored by you,"* or *"I lied because you never believe me anyway!"* And maybe it's also true: cheating often happens when you don't feel valued or loved in a relationship. However, it's important to recognize that cheating is always the perpetrator's fault. If you feel ignored, devalued, and unloved, the best solution is to make your partner aware of your feelings and talk about them.

The cheating partner should then ask themselves what factors "drove" them to cheat. Monotony in the relationship? Lack of love? Feelings of inferiority and personal devaluation? It is necessary to identify the source of the suffering and resolve the problem at its root. If a lack of love is identified as the root cause, there may be no point in trying to repair the relationship. If, on the other hand, the problem is monotony, there are many things that can be done to revive the relationship and it's worth trying.

## 2. Attune

By this point, the cheating partner should have realized the extent of their actions, accepted blame and responsibility, and had a firm intention to breathe new life into the relationship. How do you avoid making the same mistakes you made in the past? How can the relationship really take a different turn?

Think for a moment about what Gottman did when he saw his wife in distress: he put aside what he was doing and gave priority to his partner's well-being. This is the quality that every relationship should have. If Gottman had not offered his wife support that day, she would probably not have felt comfortable asking for it in the future. Instead, showing your partner that you can count on each other creates a bond, a deep friendship, and a sense of solidarity. After all, being together means supporting each other through the good times and the bad.

In their book *What Makes Love Last*, Gottman and his colleague Silver (2013) suggest a series of exercises to help you question your own level of trust in the couple and, more importantly, try to rebuild it.

Some of these are similar to the role-playing exercises we suggested in the previous section. Others, however, focus precisely on the present reality and the feelings of the partners. For example, one exercise simply provides a list of qualities and asks the participants to put a tick next to the quality they think describes their partner. Some of these qualities are:

- intelligent
- imaginative
- creative
- attractive
- playful

- reliable
- likable
- attentive
- cheerful
- honest

Although it may seem strange to think about your partner's qualities after a betrayal, this exercise is more useful than it seems. In fact, when you are arguing, you tend to forget the reasons why you loved your partner and focus only on the negative qualities. This (unconscious) behavior can make you see everything in black and white and make reconciliation difficult.

In short, once you have accepted that the past is the past, it's time to move on and "fall in love" again. Just like two new lovers, it is important to get to know each other, explore each other's personalities, and create a new story.

### 3. Attach

Once the guilty partner has regained our trust, understood their mistakes, and they still have positive qualities about them, we are ready to move on to phase three. To "attach" means to establish the closeness, emotional and physical intimacy, and trust that you gained after the first few months of dating. In this respect, Gottman believes that physical intimacy is a key point. That's right, happy couples have to be happy in bed too!

But again, there is no need to force it or make it unnatural. In bed, as in every area of romantic life, it all comes down to communication, or as Gottman calls it: "intimate communication."

To have good intimate communication, you must first learn to share your feelings. No one, not even your partner, can read your mind. Sometimes we wish our partner could understand us at a glance or interpret our body language, but you know what, we can't do that with them either. What you think or feel is part of your inner world, and others are not allowed to find out unless you talk about it openly. So, learn to express what you feel, what you want, and what bothers you in clear and honest words.

Secondly, you can use the right words to help your partner explore their feelings. You can do this by asking open-ended questions. What am I talking about? Well, it's a technique often used in psychotherapy. When you ask the patient questions, you have to be careful not to make them answer in a certain way and give them complete freedom of choice.

Let's take an example. You and your partner are invited to a friend's birthday party. On the same day, however, your partner gets a bad fever and is unable to leave the house. So, you ask: *"You don't mind if I go anyway, do you?"* Now, this is an open-ended question because it already contains/suggests the answer the person asking it hopes to get. Phrased this way, the question suggests that you want to go to the party while your partner stays home with a fever, and you hope he won't mind. A particularly shy or fragile person might say, *"Sure, go ahead, I don't mind staying home,"* even though their feelings might tell them otherwise.

On the other hand, if you want to leave your interlocutor free to choose, you need to make sure that the question is not too "intrusive." For example, the correct alternative in the scenario above would be *"How are you feeling? What would you like to do tonight?"* Your partner might answer that they just want to go to sleep and that they do not mind if you go to the party. Or maybe your partner doesn't really feel like being alone, has a high fever, and can't prepare dinner. I mean, that's just an example. But you get the point.

The third and final skill to develop to ensure a healthy and lasting relationship is certainly empathy. We have talked about this before, where we explain that insecure-avoidants tend not to be very empathetic individuals, and additionally where we introduce mirror neurons. In short, if you want to relate to your partner, you need to take an active interest and value their feelings and thoughts.

As you may have noticed, the relationship qualities and "skills" we have been talking about do not just concern those who have an anxious type of attachment, but they concern everyone. All couples need to be actively involved in setting boundaries, making concessions, and building trust. When we begin to see our partner as our friend, as a member of our family, there will be no more mind games, insecurities, push and pull, distance, and everything else that can damage a relationship.

And if you think psychology has exhausted its resources to help you, think again: the road to self-improvement is still long and bumpy. In fact, it may not even have begun yet.

# Chapter Six

# Self-Healing and Empowerment

## 6.1 Silencing the inner critic

What comes to mind when I say "talking cricket"? Have I triggered a memory for you? The talking cricket is a very famous character that appears in Carlo Collodi's book *The Adventures of Pinocchio: Story of a Puppet,"* which later became the famous Walt Disney cartoon.

Many of us may be familiar with this cartoon. It's about the adventures of Pinocchio, a puppet made by the carpenter Geppetto, and essentially his journey of development and maturation into a real boy.

Back to our talking cricket, or Jiminy Cricket as it is called in the cartoon. When we were children, he may have seemed like nothing more than a little friend of Pinocchio, dressed as a gentleman in a suit and tie. But on closer inspection, the cricket turns out to be something quite different: he is the voice of Pinocchio's own conscience, intervening at crucial moments in the story to suggest the right choices. In a way, one could say that the cricket is nothing less than a projection of Pinocchio himself and also a fundamental character for the unfolding and completion of the story.

So, why are we talking about Jiminy Cricket? Because he represents a phenomenon that many of us are familiar with: the inner voice. Have you ever, in moments of reflection, had a conversation with yourself? Perhaps just before you go shopping, you repeat to yourself: *"6 eggs, a packet of pasta, half a kilo of tomatoes, a salad..."* Or just before you have to make a presentation at university or at work, you may mentally rehearse your speech and repeat the words you are going to say out loud.

But here's something interesting: not everyone has an inner dialogue. In an experiment with 30 people, only a quarter of them experienced an inner monologue, and those who did still found it difficult to put the content of that monologue into words (Hurlburt, 2011).

Yet inner dialogue has many advantages. Think of memory consolidation: repeating a university lesson to yourself helps you remember it better, as does repeating the shopping list or anything else. It also has a great motivational component, which is what interests us most: by repeating positive phrases to yourself, you can direct your thinking toward a certain mindset.

That's right, developing a positive inner dialogue can motivate you in many areas of life. I use the word "develop" because what we say to ourselves is often automatic and unconscious. If you're a pessimistic person, in times of stress, you might say to yourself: *"I can't do this," "I'm going to fail,"* or *"I am a loser."* Conversely, if you are an optimistic person, you might say positive phrases to yourself: *"I can do it," "I must not give up,"* and so on.

The question is: what can you do if you find that your inner monologue is mainly negative and harmful? Perhaps you have had a particularly stressful day and find yourself having bad thoughts, feeling down, and depressed.

The first thing to remember is that the type of thought you have is determined by what you are focusing on at that moment. Let's take an example. You and your partner have taken a break and now, after almost two weeks of not speaking to each other, you meet again. As you prepare to leave the house, the usual negative thoughts come up: *"This break was useless, we'll fight again," "I won't be able to cope with my anxiety attacks," "I'll make mistakes again."* Do these phrases sound familiar?

If you find yourself having the same negative thoughts you had at certain times in your life, you are focusing on those past moments and replaying them in your mind. This phenomenon, also known as **rumination**, does nothing more than make you mentally associate a present event with a past event rather than giving you the opportunity to start afresh. It is, therefore, important to learn to separate the two events by focusing on elements that you have not previously paid attention to.

For example, in a situation where you meet your boyfriend again after a few weeks, try to shift your attention to the benefits of your break, your partner's positive qualities, and what you have in common. Try a **visualization** exercise. Close your eyes and try to visualize a good memory you have with him, almost like a film. Once you have identified the memory, try to remember all the details: the place you were, the weather, the atmosphere, and the other people present. As you do this, you may remember the clothes you were wearing, the sequence of events, and other details previously unknown to you.

Visualization is, in fact, another facet of the inner monologue, if not an integral and fundamental element. To understand it better, if visualization creates the images of the film, then monologue creates the subtitles. However, only together do these two elements create the complete experience we have when we go to the cinema, especially when the film is in a foreign language!

Similarly, when the images of this beautiful memory appear, try to describe them in your mind. This will give a new voice to your thoughts, and you will "connect" new sentences to the upcoming meeting: *"Maybe he will show up with a bouquet of flowers, as he did that day three years ago," "I will be able to have a calm and constructive conversation, as I did in the first period of our relationship."*

In short, think of the inner dialogue as a friend who motivates you and helps you through difficult times. Think of the talking cricket: it certainly didn't tell Pinocchio how silly he was at times, but rather helped him to improve and grow.

## 6.2 Practicing self-compassion

We have talked at length about the importance of understanding others, empathizing with their feelings, and developing the right amount of empathy to enable us to have meaningful relationships. But what about the relationship we should have with ourselves? We tend to be our own worst critics and enemies.

But, you see, I am not alone in saying this. It seems that the relationship we had with our parents as children, and the kind of attachment we developed, also influences the kind of relationship we will have with ourselves. If our childhood caregiver treats us with love, respect, and gentleness, we learn that this is how everyone should treat us. We learn that we are people worthy of love and respect, and this is how we will treat ourselves in the future (Neff & McGhee, 2010).

Remember the internal working models we spoke about at the beginning? They are an image, a structure of the world that we unconsciously internalize, determined by the first relationship we have with the world (the one we have with our parents).

Similarly, if we develop an insecure-avoidant or anxious attachment, our mental structure will teach us that we are unworthy of love, are always wrong, and therefore we cannot love others (in the case of insecure-avoidant), or that others cannot love us (in the case of insecure-anxious).

In short, self-compassion is closely linked to the type of attachment we develop. The insecure-anxious, in particular, often tend to see themselves in a bad light, see more faults than qualities in themselves, and generally have a poor opinion of themselves.

However, we often underestimate the impact that low self-esteem and a lack of self-love can have on our mental health and happiness. First of all, try to imagine the kind of inner monologue these people can have... that's right, a very negative one. In fact, these people think not only about the negative elements of the world but also about themselves. They are convinced that all or most of the bad things that happen in their lives are their fault.

*"If my partner doesn't answer the phone, it's my fault: I nag him too much."*

*"If my partner flirts with other girls, it's my fault: I am not enough for him."*

*"If our relationship breaks down, it is usually my fault: I never change."*

As you can imagine, this kind of thinking is very problematic. Firstly, by blaming yourself, you are only undermining your self-esteem and potentially causing mental health problems. In fact, self-criticism has long been correlated with problems such as eating disorders, personality disorders, and depression (Werner et al., 2019). It's quite simple: if we don't like ourselves, we will have a bad relationship with the world.

Secondly, if we attribute all the problems in the relationship to ourselves, we will think that our partner is never wrong, and we will never feel the need to "correct" them. We have seen, however, that an insecure-anxious and an insecure-avoidant are like different jigsaw pieces: no matter how hard we try to make them fit, there will always be a corner that sticks out. One thing is certain: if you don't identify the matrix of the problem (and only attribute it to yourself), you will never solve it.

The first step in developing more compassion for yourself is to identify your own self-criticism. What do you say to yourself in times of difficulty? Do you tend to take it out on others or on yourself? This is the time to use the visualization exercise described in the previous paragraph. Instead of reliving a happy memory with your partner, try to mentally go through the stages of your argument. Are you still convinced that you were the only one to blame?

Here is another concept to learn and internalize: you are not the negative emotions you feel. Psychological suffering, pain, and low self-esteem are all side effects of being in the world; it is only when we relate to the world and to others that we can feel bad, if we do so with the wrong mindset. If you feel overwhelmed by these feelings, try to focus on the "here and now" by trying the breathing exercises we talked about earlier.

In fact, in order to think as well as to feel emotions, happiness, and pain, it is necessary for the right amount of oxygen to reach the brain. If you learn to control your breathing (gradually slowing it down), you will also prevent thoughts from crowding your brain.

For example, while you are sitting cross-legged and concentrating on your breathing, try to slow down the rhythm of your breathing. Breathe in deeply and count to three: one, two, three. Now, hold your breath for a second. Exhale counting to four: one, two, three, four. Now, pause for a second or two. Then, repeat again. In this way, your breathing follows the duration of your counting and gradually slows down. During this exercise, you will notice a sense of calm and peace that you have not felt for a long time. So, what happened to your self-criticism?

# 6.3 Daily rituals for healing

In everyday life, there are many practices that psychologists and therapists around the world recommend to improve your health and your relationship with yourself. Let's look at some of them together.

Have you ever kept a secret diary? Many children/adolescents do, especially when they enter that stage of life where they feel misunderstood. So, they take a small notebook and write down the thoughts that accompany their days.

If this sounds like a childish thing to do, think again. This practice is called **journaling,** and it consists of putting your thoughts and feelings on paper in order to understand them better. And I'll tell you more: if you start this practice as a child, you'll learn to know your feelings right from the start. A recent experiment tested the effect of journaling on middle school children, who then declared that the exercise helped them to overcome their fears and anxieties (Crawford, 2021). The author of the same experiment explained that the practice is part of mindfulness techniques and helps people understand themselves better in the long term.

Try to remember the worst day you have had in the last month. First, identify the reason. (e.g., *"I felt bad after a fight with my boyfriend"*). Then, try to remember the sequence of events (e.g., *"I found out that day that my boyfriend had lied to me about something in our relationship..."*). Okay, what about the feelings you had that day? Surely, you must have felt anger, resentment, and frustration. But can you recall the specifics? Now that the anger of the moment has passed, you find it difficult to remember the sequence of your thoughts during or immediately after the event, the resolutions you had in mind, your impressions, and your feelings.

This is where the practice of journaling is useful. It allows you to analyze your state of mind at the moment when you are most vulnerable (for example, during an argument) and, above all, it allows you to return to these pages later and get to know the person you are when you are fragile and vulnerable.

In this way, you don't have to relive a difficult moment to get in touch with those feelings; you can just read them. Here is an extract from Ann's diary, which she let me read after her relationship with Max ended:

*"I just wish I could get my anger out somehow. I feel like I could explode. I wish I had a baseball bat to scream and smash things. I feel the tears flooding my brain. Is it anger? Fear of being alone? A sense of defeat? I don't know. I know I have failed. All that is left is hatred and a shattered life. I have nothing left, no one. I wish Max would really disappear, quietly.*

*That any reconciliation would not cloud my mind again. It's like an hourglass: when all the grains of sand reach the bottom, it turns over and starts again."*

That's how Ann felt a few months before she and Max broke up. She confided in me that she was in disbelief every time she reread those words: how could they have been created in her brain, the same brain that had now found the strength to end all that suffering? And yet those words had been hers.

Sure, a good dose of self-analysis is always helpful, but many daily rituals also involve giving your mind and body the right amount of relaxation and rest. And the good news is that there are many ways to relax.

I am sure that each of us, in our own way, lives a chaotic and busy life—some due to studies, some due to work, and some due to taking care of our families. In short, sometimes there just seems to be no room for a moment to yourself. From now on, however, I would like to urge you to set aside just twenty minutes a day for your physical and mental well-being.

First, think of an activity that inspires you at that moment, such as a warm bath, a walk alone or with a friend, listening to music, yoga, or exercise. In short, an activity that you would like to do often but cannot find the time for.

On the other hand, if you are looking for a specific relaxation technique to do during your daily twenty-minute break, I recommend **progressive muscle relaxation**.

Invented more than 100 years ago by Edmund Jacobson, progressive muscle relaxation involves voluntarily contracting one group of muscles at a time—think of the muscles in your arms or legs—and then suddenly relaxing them. The action of contracting and relaxing the muscles in succession has the effect of intensifying the feeling of relaxation that occurs immediately after the contraction: blood pressure drops, the pulse slows down, and breathing becomes calmer.

This technique not only produces relaxation at the moment it is performed but also helps you to become more aware of your body. In fact, the positive effects on a larger scale (emotional improvement, stress management, etc.) are already visible after 8–12 weeks. As you do the exercise muscularly, you also acquire the ability to do it mentally, without having to visibly contract your muscles. For stress management, you would do the same thing: identify the stress matrix, focus on it intensely, and then let it go, much like you relax a muscle after a contraction.

Both journaling and progressive relaxation are excellent practices for those who, like you, want to find moments of peace and quiet while learning more about their own minds and bodies.

# Conclusion

We have reached the final pages of this book and the end of our journey together. In fact, I see it as the end of a personal journey that began many years ago when I started studying insecure attachment. However, like any good journey, when you reach your destination, you don't simply close a chapter of your life but bring with you a whole series of experiences and lessons.

Similarly, we have learned to redefine the word "normal." Usually, when we talk about mental health problems, we look at those who suffer from them in a bit of an ugly duckling way. On one side we have the "normal," and on the other side we have the depressed, the anxious, the schizophrenic, the obsessive, and so on and so forth. Through this book, however, we have learned that every single individual on the face of the earth falls into at least one of three categories: the secure, the insecure-avoidant, and the insecure-anxious.

We have also learned that much, if not everything, depends on the first interactions we have with the world through our parents. In particular, if our primary attachment figure alternated between an affectionate style and an unfriendly and grumpy one, we were likely to develop an insecure-anxious type of attachment. But, mind you, this is not an obstacle or a disorder and is nothing more than a particular way of relating to the world. For this reason, it is necessary to know our own needs and requirements, as well as looking for someone who celebrates and respects them.

At the same time, getting to know yourself in depth means creating the conditions in your life that will allow you to live it to the fullest, happily and without regret. For instance, if Ann once thought she was the worst person in the world, but now she couldn't be happier with herself and her achievements. She now has a man she loves and who loves her for who she is. She has learned to respect her partner's boundaries and to get him to respect hers. In short, they fit together like two pieces of the same puzzle: they complement each other.

This is not to say that we necessarily need to find our own missing piece of the puzzle. Often, the people in our lives are fleeting, and what really matters is finding the right balance with ourselves. Day by day, we need to take note of our inner workings, what makes us feel good, and what is better avoided.

In these final pages, I would also like to tell you briefly about a very famous novel that I personally loved very much. It is *The Catcher in the Rye* by J.D. Salinger. I remember reading this book in Maine just before I moved to Seattle, and somehow, it was this reading that inspired me to take on the adventure of moving to a new city, far away from home.

The book is about Holden Caulfield, a bright young teenager who recounts some events from the previous year. He talks about how he was expelled from the school he attended for lack of commitment to his studies, his classmates, and one of his teachers who urged him to study and not waste his talent. As the story unfolds, we also learn that Holden lost a brother to illness. However, Holden still cannot believe that his brother is really gone, and this reveals a great suffering that has contributed to making him the person he is.

Among the characters in this book is Phoebe, his younger sister, only 10 years old, for whom Holden has great respect. He speaks of Phoebe as a wise person, much wiser than he is, and in fact, she is the only person in his family he visits after he is expelled from school.

So why am I telling you about this book? Because I believe that the key word in this work is "growth," a word that also encapsulates the deeper meaning of our book on attachment. Despite the expulsion from school, the lack of friends (Holden is a reserved and critical boy), the awareness of the disappointment his expulsion will bring to his parents, and the enormous pain that Holden feels and will always feel over the death of his brother, Holden grows and faces the succession of events that make up his life without ever retreating.

It is, in fact, a novel of formation, in which the various elements that make up the book are also those that determine the individual development of the character. But isn't that the way everyone's life works? If certain events (different in each of our lives) had not happened a few years ago, we would not be the people we are today. Remember, every experience, negative or positive, contributes to the development of our personality, our inner world, our intellect, our emotionality…

This is also what is meant by the concept of "growth mindset," in the words of Carol Dweck, a famous American psychologist: *"…this growth mindset is based on the belief that your basic qualities are things you can cultivate through your efforts."* The events, people, and situations that shape your life are not elements to be passively absorbed. On the contrary, you must see them as means by which you can grow, develop, and change.

In fact, one of the cornerstones of the growth mindset is precisely the principle of "learning through experience." Think of Ann: if she had never been exposed to someone like Max, she would never have discovered this "problematic" and negative side of herself. She would never have learned that an avoidant partner made her an anxious, jealous, insecure person. So, through the suffering that this relationship caused her, Ann identified a latent "problem," confronted it, and eventually resolved it. This is the process of growth I am talking about. It's only by facing your inner demons that you learn to confront and defeat them.

Of course, the process of growth is not immediate and automatic. It's not by confronting one problem that one solves them all. Rather, it is an ongoing journey. Even our parents, whom we think of as adults par excellence, are still learning from their mistakes, still suffering, and still growing, day by day.

This concept is also masterfully expressed in Salinger's book and is hidden in the title itself. What is *The Catcher in the Rye*? The title comes from a 1782 Scottish ballad by Robert Burns called *"Comin' thro' the Rye,"* The meaning of the phrase has always been a mystery, but some people think it refers to the field of rye through which Jenny (a character mentioned in the ballad) walks, soaking wet (perhaps because of the dew?).

In any case, the expression appears in the book—as well as in the title—when Holden's sister asks him, *"What do you want to be when you grow up?"* and Holden replies: *"... I'm standing on the edge of some crazy cliff. What I have to do, I have to catch everybody if they start to go over the cliff—I mean if they're running and they don't look where*

*they're going, I have to come out from somewhere and catch them. That's all
I'd do all day. I'd just be the catcher in the rye and all."*

So, what does Holden want to do? Protect all those who were
children like him, prevent them from making his own mistakes?
Does he want to catch them before they sink into the abyss of
suffering? This is not possible, and Holden knows it. At the end
of the book, he reveals that he doesn't know how he will behave
when he goes back to school, whether he will study this time or
not. In short, Holden himself is still a "victim" of the inexorable
mechanism of life, of the succession of events from which one
cannot escape, but which happen for a very specific reason: to
make one grow.

And so all that remains for these children is to learn to stand up
for themselves, as we are all destined to do: accepting victories
and defeats as integral parts of the wonderful experience called
life.

# Thank You

I'm deeply appreciative that you decided to purchase my book.

With so many options available, it means a lot that you chose mine. I'm truly grateful for your decision to read it through to its conclusion.

Before we part ways, I have a small favor to ask. Would you be willing to leave a review on the platform?

Your review is invaluable and is one of the simplest yet most impactful ways you can support independent authors like myself.

Your insights are crucial in guiding me to create books that are truly beneficial to you.

All the best,

Elara

## >> Leave a review on Amazon US <<

## >> Leave a review on Amazon UK <<

# Bibliography

American Psychiatric Association. (2022). Anxiety disorders. In *Diagnostic and statistical manual of mental disorders* (5th ed., text rev.)

Capobianco, M., & Cerniglia, L. (2018). Case Report: Evaluation strategies and cognitive intervention: the case of a monovular twin child affected by selective mutism. *F1000Research, 7.*

Chen, Y., Li, R., Zhang, P., & Liu, X. (2020). The Moderating Role of State Attachment Anxiety and Avoidance Between Social Anxiety and Social Networking Sites Addiction. *Psychological Reports, 123*(3), 633-647. https://doi.org/10.1177/0033294118823178

Cowen, A. S., & Keltner, D. (2017). Self-report captures 27 distinct categories of emotion bridged by continuous gradients. *Proceedings of the National Academy of Sciences, 114*(38), E7900-E7909.

Crawford, A., Sellman, E., & Joseph, S. (2021). Journaling: A more mindful approach to researching a mindfulness-based intervention in a junior school. *International Journal of Qualitative Methods. 20.* https://doi.org/10.1177/16094069211014771

Ein-Dor, T., Mikulincer, M., Doron, G., & Shaver, P. R. (2010). The attachment paradox: How can so many of us (the insecure ones) have no adaptive advantages? *Perspectives on Psychological Science, 5*(2), 123-141.

Ekman, P., Friesen, W. V., O'Sullivan, M., Chan, A.,

Diacoyanni-Tarlatzis, I., Heider, K., Krause, R., LeCompte, W. A., Pitcairn, T., Ricci-Bitti, P. E., Scherer, K., Tomita, M., & Tzavaras, A. (1987). Universals and cultural differences in the judgments of facial expressions of emotion. *Journal of Personality and Social Psychology, 53*(4), 712–717. https://doi.org/10.1037/0022-3514.53.4.712

Gallese, V., Fadiga, L., Fogassi, L., & Rizzolatti, G. (1996). Action recognition in the premotor cortex. *Brain, 119*(2), 593–609. https://doi.org/10.1093/brain/119.2.593

Garner, A. R., & Stuart, G. L. (2023). Integrating mindfulness and acceptance into traditional cognitive behavioral therapy during the COVID-19 pandemic: A case study of an adult man with generalized anxiety disorder. *Clinical Case Studies, 22*(2), 120–137. https://doi.org/10.1177/15346501221123568

Goleman, D. (1995). *Emotional intelligence.* Bantam Books.

Gottman, J. M., & Silver, N. (2013). *What makes love last?: How to build trust and avoid betrayal.* Simon & Schuster Paperbacks.

Harris, R. (2022). *The happiness trap: Stop struggling, start living.* Robinson.

Hart, J., Nailling, E., Bizer, G. Y., & Collins, C. K. (2015). Attachment theory as a framework for explaining engagement with Facebook. *Personality and Individual Differences, 77*, 33-40.

Hayes, S. C. (2004). Acceptance and commitment therapy, relational frame theory, and the third wave of behavioral and cognitive therapies. *Behavior Therapy, 35*(4), 639-665.

Hurlburt, R. T. (2011). *Investigating pristine inner experience: Moments of truth.* Cambridge University Press.

Izard, C. E., Woodburn, E. M., Finlon, K. J., Krauthamer-Ewing, E. S., Grossman, S. R., & Seidenfeld, A. (2011). Emotion knowledge, emotion utilization, and emotion regulation. *Emotion Review*, *3*(1), 44-52.

Jackson, C. (2022). *30% of adults say most people can be trusted | Ipsos.* Ipsos. https://www.ipsos.com/en/interpersonal-trust-across-the-world

Jiang, L., Bohle, S. L., & Roche, M. (2019). Contingent Reward Transactional Leaders as "Good Parents": Examining the Mediation Role of Attachment Insecurity and the Moderation Role of Meaningful Work. *Journal of Business and Psychology*, *34*(4), 519-537.

Jinyao, Y., Xiongzhao, Z., Auerbach, R. P., Gardiner, C. K., Lin, C., Yuping, W., & Shuqiao, Y. (2012). Insecure attachment as a predictor of depressive and anxious symptomology. *Depression and Anxiety*, *29*(9), 789–796. https://doi.org/10.1002/da.21953

Kampourakis, K., and McCain, K. The Psychology of (Un)Certainty, *Uncertainty: How It Makes Science Advance* (New York, 2019; online edn, Oxford Academic, 24 Oct. 2019), https://doi.org/10.1093/oso/9780190871666.003.0002, accessed 5 Dec. 2023

Koskina, N., & Giovazolias, T., (2010) The Effect of Attachment Insecurity in the Development of Eating Disturbances across Gender: The Role of Body Dissatisfaction, *The Journal of Psychology, 144*:5, 449-471, DOI: 10.1080/00223980.2010.496651

Lee, G. Y., & Kisilevsky, B. S. (2014). Fetuses respond to father's voice but prefer mother's voice after birth. *Developmental Psychobiology*, *56*(1), 1-11.

Neff, K. D., & McGehee, P. (2010). Self-compassion and psychological resilience among adolescents and young adults. *Self and Identity*, *9*(3), 225-240.

Nummenmaa, L., Glerean, E., Hari, R., & Hietanen, J. K. (2014). Bodily maps of emotions. *Proceedings of the National Academy of Sciences of the United States of America*, *111*(2), 646-651.

Overall, N. C., Fletcher, G. J., Simpson, J. A., & Fillo, J. (2015). Attachment insecurity, biased perceptions of romantic partners' negative emotions, and hostile relationship behavior. *Journal of Personality and Social Psychology*, *108*(5), 730–749. https://doi.org/10.1037/a0038987

Peterson, C. (2021). What is your earliest memory? It depends. *Memory*, *29*(6), 811-822.

Qiu, J. (2006). Epigenetics: Unfinished symphony. *Nature*, *441*(7090), 143+. https://link.gale.com/apps/doc/A185450297/AONE?u=anon~dfa3dd29&sid=googleScholar&xid=0b1ee81a

Shaver, P. R., & Mikulincer, M. (2007). Adult attachment strategies and the regulation of emotion. *Handbook of emotion regulation*, *446*, 465.

Siegel, D. (2018, May 21). *A framework for cultivating integration*. PsychAlive. https://www.psychalive.org/framework-cultivating-integration/

Stöven, L. M., & Herzberg, P. Y. (2021). Relationship 2.0: A systematic review of associations between the use of social network sites and attachment style. *Journal of Social and Personal Relationships*, *38*(3), 1103-1128. https://doi.org/10.1177/0265407520982671

Tennov, D. (1998). *Love and limerence: The experience of being in love*.

Hayes

Elara Hayes

Elara Hayes

Scarborough House.

Werner, A. M., Tibubos, A. N., Rohrmann, S., & Reiss, N. (2019). The clinical trait self-criticism and its relation to psychopathology: A systematic review–Update. *Journal of Affective Disorders, 246*, 530-547.

World Health Organization. (n.d.). *Depressive disorder (depression)*. World Health Organization. https://www.who.int/news-room/fact-sheets/detail/depression#:~:text=An%20estimated%20 3.8%25%20of%20the,world%20have%20depression%20 (1).